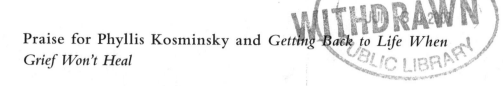
Praise for Phyllis Kosminsky and *Getting Back to Life When Grief Won't Heal*

"I have always thought of life, and grief, as a complex puzzle. When a significant person dies, there are so many pieces to ones' grief, so many missing parts. Phyllis Kosminsky offers the reader the missing pieces and makes sense out of a senseless time. This wonderful book is not only for the bereaved but for anyone who works with the bereaved, including clergy, hospice personnel, funeral directors, and, of course, all therapists."

—Helen Fitzgerald, author of *The Mourning Handbook*

"This is an extraordinary book. It provides an exceptional description of the challenges that often accompany the loss of a loved one and, more importantly, offers many resources for moving through complicated grief. I highly recommend it both for individuals struggling with bereavement and for therapists working with such clients."

—Stephen Gilligan, Ph.D., author of *The Courage to Love*

"This important book gently and clearly helps people get on with their lives and get 'unstuck' from the isolating cycle of sadness and self-blame often accompanying loss. Almost anyone struggling with grief issues will find the advice offered here to be extremely valuable."

—William Feigelman, Ph.D., author of *Chosen Children*

Getting Back to Life When Grief Won't Heal

PHYLLIS KOSMINSKY, Ph.D.

New York   Chicago   San Francisco   Lisbon   London   Madrid   Mexico City
Milan   New Delhi   San Juan   Seoul   Singapore   Sydney   Toronto

*The **McGraw·Hill** Companies*

Library of Congress Cataloging-in-Publication Data

Kosminsky, Phyllis.
　　Getting back to life when grief won't heal / Phyllis Kosminsky.
　　　　p.　　cm.
　　Includes index.
　　ISBN 0-07-146472-7
　　1. Grief—Psychological aspects.　　2. Bereavement—Psychological
aspects.　　I. Title.

BF575.G7K645　　2007
155.9'37—dc22　　　　　　　　　　　　　　　　2006027126

Song lyrics to "People" on page 27 from *Funny Girl*. Words by Bob Merrill. Music by Jule Styne. Copyright © 1963, 1964 by Bob Merrill and Jule Styne. Copyright renewed. All rights administered by Chappell & Co. International copyright secured. All rights reserved.

1 2 3 4 5 6 7 8 9 10 11 12 13 14 15　FGR/FGR　0 9 8 7 6

ISBN-13: 978-0-07-146472-7
ISBN-10:　　0-07-146472-7

McGraw-Hill books are available at special quantity discounts to use as premiums and sales promotions, or for use in corporate training programs. For more information, please write to the Director of Special Sales, Professional Publishing, McGraw-Hill, Two Penn Plaza, New York, NY 10121-2298. Or contact your local bookstore.

This book is printed on acid-free paper.

For my mother

Lucille Schoenfeld Glick

1928–1961

Contents

Acknowledgments

There are people without whom this book *could* not have been written, and those without whom I suspect it *would* not have been written.

My interest in grief and loss undoubtedly stems from my mother's death from cancer when I was nine. Many of the people I've met over the past ten years of working in this field have a similar story of early loss. Undoubtedly my desire to understand the impact of loss and how people recover from it is at heart a personal one. So in a real sense, I have to say that this book would not have been written without my mother, to whose memory it is dedicated.

My father, Jay Glick, is my rock, the solid foundation of my life. There is simply no substitute for the kind of unshakeable faith and love he has always provided me. My mom, Sandra Glick, came into my life at a time when I needed her most. A less committed woman might have balked at the prospect of raising a preadolescent girl and her three-year-old sister. She didn't, and I will always be grateful to her for that decision.

Many people helped with the writing of this book in different ways. A number of people provided substantive contributions to the text; others commented on early drafts and engaged in thoughtful discussion of the ideas presented here. Among those who helped in this way, I particularly want to thank Cindy Browning, M.S.W., and Katherine Davis, M.S.W., for the many hours they devoted to helping make this a better book. Special thanks also to my friend and teacher William Zangwill, Ph.D., who has been unfailingly generous in sharing with me his expertise as a clinician and his knowledge of EMDR.

My colleagues at the Center for Hope are a constant and essential source of clinical insight, companionable lunch conversation, and support when I need it most. The kind of clinical work that is done at the Center is all too rare, as are the people who do it. Special thanks to Anna Terleph, Susan Jacoby, Kathleen Conway, Janet Taylor, Pat Nelson, and Deirdre Lewin for their wisdom, encouragement, and friendship.

I want to thank Stephen Gilligan and the members of the self relations community in New York for all they have taught me about what it means to really listen and what it feels like to be really heard. Although we are together for only a few days a year, the sense of being connected to the extraordinary people who comprise this group is with me always.

While I was preparing the proposal for this book, I had the exceedingly good fortune to meet Susan Arellano, who became my agent. Her enthusiasm and confidence in the book and my ability to write it never flagged. Her professionalism and dedication to getting the book into the hands of readers remained constant from the beginning of the process to its completion.

I want to thank John Aherne, my editor at McGraw-Hill, for guiding me through every step of the process of making my manuscript into a book. He was just what this first-time author needed: patient, direct, and kind. My sincerest thanks to Charlie Fisher, senior project editor at McGraw-Hill, who went above and beyond in diligently incorporating my many changes and edits.

The people whose stories are presented in this book read the material included prior to publication and agreed, sometimes with revisions, to its inclusion. I have tried to represent their experiences with as much accuracy as was possible without disclosing their identities. I am deeply grateful to them for all that they have taught me about our capacity to heal from even the most devastating kinds of loss. I hope that this book fulfills their wish to provide reassurance and guidance to others who are traveling a path they know all too well.

My friends and family sustain me; they know, beyond anything I can say here, how important their loving presence is in my life. I want to thank them and also to apologize for the extended periods of absence from their company this project has required. A special thanks to my friends Phyllis Shmalo, Claudia Figari, Susan Jacoby, Steve Bittner, Carol Lowenstein, Leslie Cowen, Tamara Fuller, JoAnne Kitain, and Michael Fegin. I am especially grateful to my sister Silvia for her intelligence, humor, and fierce loyalty. I have come to rely on her steady presence in recent years and no doubt will continue to do so in the years ahead.

No one has had a closer view of the process of writing this book than my children, Lily and Eli, and it hasn't always been pretty. I have been and continue to be amazed every day by their tolerance, generosity, and adaptability in the face of domestic chaos. Most of all, I am grateful to them for the care and love they give to each other and to their parents. I can't imagine how anything, ever, could make me happier and prouder than they do.

Of the people without whom this book could not have been written, I have saved the most important for last. My husband, Jay, has been everything I've needed him to be for as long as I've known him. What I've needed most over the past two years was a partner who could help me put my thoughts on paper in a clear and cohesive manner and help me stay focused when the prospect of what I had set out to do seemed overwhelming. Beyond his skills as an insightful writer and a thorough editor, he has given freely of his wisdom, good humor, patience, and love. I am grateful to him for his help in writing this book, but even more, for bringing these qualities to every part of our life together.

CHAPTER 1

When Grief Becomes a Way of Life

~

*No one told me grief felt
so much like fear.*
—C. S. Lewis, *A Grief Observed*

If love has the power to open a heart, the loss of love can break it. The enveloping grief that accompanies the death of a loved one is a subject many have tried to capture in words but, like love itself, is something that cannot be fully understood other than through direct experience. Love stretches our heart to the limits of what it can hold, and grief, to the limits of what it can bear.

There is no way around the pain that accompanies the death of someone we love. Sorrow saps our energy, making it difficult to accomplish the simplest tasks. The return to a fully active and engaged life seems a distant possibility. We may wonder whether we can ever be the same, even as we struggle to remember who we were before our loss. As C. S. Lewis observed, the experience of grief can produce emotions that feel very much like fear: physically and emotionally we may feel as though we are in peril, as if our very survival is in question. Our instinct is to try to regain control, to find what we have lost. But what we have lost is truly gone; there is no replacement, and at least for now there is no consolation.

Yet, despite the immensity of the experience, the pain of losing a loved one is a blow from which most people do recover. Over time, the fear and emptiness start to subside. Harsh and painful emotions gradually are softened by memories of what was and thoughts of what may lie ahead. With the support of family and friends, and perhaps a good therapist, acceptance of death is followed ultimately by reengagement in life, and people move on.

But not always. Sometimes, and more often than generally is recognized, people do not make a healthy recovery from loss. For many months or years, they find themselves pulled down by the powerful gravity of grief, drawn inexorably back to the same dark place of fear and sadness. I see people like this in my office every day, people who are experiencing a grief so intense and unrelenting that they can barely express it, much less heal from it. For a variety of reasons, they simply cannot stop thinking about the person they've lost. They mentally rerun their lives together. They replay the death again and again. Thinking about the past evokes unbearably painful emotions, but so does thinking about the future.

People in this situation have described it to me as a feeling of being stuck. Instead of getting better, they seem to be getting nowhere. Something is preventing them from moving past their loss. Let's look at what it means to be stuck and how it is that some people come to find themselves in the grip of unrelenting grief.

Getting Stuck

MOURNING IS THE PROCESS through which we recover from the emotional wound inflicted by the death of someone we love. As with a physical trauma or illness, some emotional healing occurs spontaneously. We are remarkable beings in this regard, each of us the product of millions of years of successful evolution and adaptation. Our minds and bodies are built to recover from illness and injury. But as we all know from experience, some illnesses and injuries, if left untreated, overwhelm our bodies' healing capacities and continue to get worse. Similarly, some grief is so intense or so complicated that it overwhelms our mind's ability to heal. Instead of proceeding steadily toward recovery, the mourning process falters or breaks down entirely, and the emotional and physical symptoms of grief become chronic and can even intensify. What does it feel like to be stuck in grief? Here's how it was described to me by Suzanne, a sixty-two-year old grandmother, a year after her mother's death:

> I feel like I'm on a wheel, going around and around. I'm just not getting any better. I'm so frustrated. It's been a year, but it still feels like it happened yesterday. I still cry out for my mother. I wait for her to call. I think of going to see her. I just can't stop thinking about her.

Suzanne is not alone in her feelings. Perhaps one out of three people experiencing a close personal loss find themselves similarly stuck at one point or another, unable to move on through mourning and adapt to their changed life. In Suzanne's case, despite the fact that she has children of her own, and her children now have children, she just can't get her own mother out of her head. It's not just that she thinks often of her mother or that she misses her mother: Suzanne is consumed by thoughts of her mother.

I meet many people whose experience with grief is similar to Suzanne's, and I hear from many others who know people like Suzanne and want to help but don't know how. It may be a parent who has died, a spouse, a sibling, or even a very close friend. Whatever the nature of the relationship that was lost, the feelings people describe are much the same. People who believe they should be feeling better are feeling worse; they feel frustrated and increasingly are absorbed in thoughts of what was and what might have been. In their own minds, they simply are not the person they were before, and they have begun to fear they never will be again.

People stuck in their grief sometimes ask me, "Am I going crazy?" or "Is my situation hopeless?" Having witnessed the recovery of hundreds of grieving people, I would say that almost always the answer to both questions is no. Most people, even those who believe they never will recover, do. No matter how wounded and lost they feel, most people eventually find a way to come to terms with their loss and find new meaning in their lives. I see it happen all the time. Still, by the very nature of grief, there are times it may seem an impossible task. Grief, after all, is a response to loss, the ultimate loss, and, more than any human experience, something over which we ultimately are powerless. But we are not powerless in how we respond to it. Like anything that frightens us, we can move toward grief rather than trying to avoid it: we can let ourselves fall into the truth of what we have lost rather than trying to resist it.

Willingness to face the truth of what we have lost and to experience the full range of our feelings about the person who has died is the beginning of healing. It is also, more often than not, the beginning of a fuller appreciation of who we are and what we're capable of becoming. What I often observe is that people who are able, on their own or with help, to confront and understand their feelings about the loss of a loved one discover in the process that they are stronger and more resilient than they had imagined themselves to be. The more they learn about themselves, the more they seem able to believe that they can get through their pain and move on with their lives.

Our New Understanding of Mourning

As a culture, we have come a long way in our common understanding of grief and loss. When I was growing up in the sixties, people dealing with the death of someone close to them were pretty much expected to get through it on their own. Certainly it was assumed that friends and family would help out, bring food, lend a sympathetic ear. But nobody read (or wrote) books about getting over the loss of a loved one, and few people sought help outside of a small circle of friends and family.

That's the way I remember it, anyway. I was nine when my mother died, and no other event in my life has affected me as profoundly, or likely ever will. As with most people I speak to who lost a parent when they were young, my mother's death defined me. It influenced my feelings about myself, my expectations of life, and my ability and willingness to form relationships. After my mother died, people were kind, but no one knew how to talk to me about what I was feeling. There was never any mention of seeking outside help or otherwise dealing in a serious way with all the thoughts and fears of a nine-year-old girl who had just lost her mother. My father tried once or twice to talk to me, but I knew that he was sad too, and I didn't want to make him sadder. Like most children in this situation, I understood that it was important for the adults around me to believe that I was OK, and that's how I tried to appear. From what I've heard from other people my age who lost a parent early in life, my experience is far from unique.

In my work with grieving individuals and families, I have come to appreciate just how much things have changed for the better since I was a child. Generally, people are more conscious of their own and other people's need for support after a significant loss and of the need to express their feelings and to encourage children to do the same. There are books, TV shows, and Internet sites about death and grieving, and people seek out this information and make use of it.

Thanks to these resources, many people who experience a loss understand something of what they are in for. They understand that they are facing a process and that it will not be quick or without pain. Because they have read about it, or someone has talked to them, many mourners expect that they may go through a period of denial ("I can't believe he's gone") and then confrontation of the full range of feelings ("Sometimes he was hard to live with"), and that they eventually will come to accept and accommodate their loss ("I'll never forget him, but I don't want to stop living").

While simplified, this is a pretty accurate description of normal grief. As people move through mourning, they begin to engage in healing tasks—acknowledging, experiencing, and accepting the loss of the relationship and all that it meant to them. As a person's attention and energy are less involved with mourning, a greater share of personal resources becomes available to invest in life. A distinct shift in focus takes place. Day-to-day life is less about what happened in the past and more about what's happening in the moment. Thinking about the person who has died is as likely to bring a smile as a tear. The mourner gradually becomes less absorbed with thoughts about what death has taken and more conscious of what has been gained from having had that person in his or her life. People experiencing normal grief eventually come to a point at which they again are able to enjoy the things that used to give them pleasure and explore new ways of finding meaning and satisfaction in their lives. Like an ever-widening passageway, mourning begins in the dark, narrow isolation of intense emotional pain and gradually broadens into the light of new experience and relationships. For people who have lost a loved one, the realization that they can go on—often accompanied by the sense that this is what their loved one would have wanted for them—helps give them the energy and the courage to make a new start.

Even when it is going "well," of course, mourning is rarely straightforward. People don't just march right through the process of mourning. They have good days and bad days. They make progress and have setbacks. Almost anyone who grieves has moments of doubt. At some point, almost everyone experiences frustration with their inability to get hold of their emotions. With time, patience, and support, they move forward again and reach a new level of understanding and adjustment. They may face other setbacks, but experience tells them that these too will be temporary. Deep down, they know that they are healing and that they are moving away from their isolation and pain toward reengagement with the world.

Then there are people like Suzanne, whose grief is not unfolding in the way they, and others, expected it to. They may have turned to the literature on grief, and it doesn't seem to be written for them. In fact, the more they read, the more frustrated they become, because they just do not seem to be healing the way people typically heal. They wonder why they are not "on schedule" in their recovery process. Some begin to feel that if their grief isn't following a normal pattern, there must be something not quite normal about *them*.

They are right to question, but wrong to blame themselves or think that they are in some way lacking or even a little crazy. While the majority of people experience what we have come to understand as a typical mourning process, many do not. And by many I mean that each year for hundreds of thousands of people in this country who experience a close personal loss, mourning does not proceed normally.[1] Why not?

It's clear to me, and I hope it will be to you as you read this book, that there are many reasons people experience prolonged, intense grief, but the explanation is not that they are by nature weaker or less courageous than other people confronting loss. Suzanne is a resilient, positive woman who finds pleasure in her family and her work. She has no shortage of courage, strength, or insight. It is simply that something is interfering with her healing, preventing her from moving through the stages of mourning to recovery. Her mourning, and the mourning of so many others I see, is what experts in the field of bereavement call "complicated mourning." For Suzanne and so many others, time will not be enough to heal the wounds inflicted by the loss of a loved one. They are stuck, and to get unstuck they will first have to find out which memories, feelings, and emotions are standing in the way of their recovery.

What Do We Know About Complicated Mourning?

TWENTY YEARS AGO, in the first major study of its kind, Harvard researchers interviewed hundreds of widows and widowers to see how they were adjusting to their loss.[2] One thing the researchers were after was to understand how the quality of a marriage affected recovery from grief. What they expected to find was that the men and women whose suffering was most acute would be those who had had the most compatible, loving, and happy relationships. After all, they theorized, these were the people who had experienced the loss of not just a mate, but in many cases the love of their lives, their best friend and soul mate. The study's findings, however, indicated something very different. The people who were having the roughest time were those whose relationships had been less than ideal.

This is not to say that the survivor of a warm, loving relationship experiences any less grief than the survivor of a tempestuous relationship. Far from it. It's just that that person's *recovery* from grief is likely to be easier, and it isn't hard to see why. One inference of the Harvard study, and something I see confirmed every day, is that love can be a great source of strength as a person moves through mourning. If a mourner was in a loving relationship, relatively uncomplicated by excessive anger, guilt, or resentment, he or she is able to draw on that love freely to foster healing. But when love is closely tied to other powerful emotions, or to memories that are confusing and painful, it can become impossible to draw on that love without dredging up parts of the past that the mourner wants to forget. This is one of the ways that mourning gets complicated and people get stuck.

In the Harvard study, one year after the death of a spouse, individuals whose marriages had been more troubled reported higher levels of tension and anxiety, and their emotional problems were accompanied by physical problems ranging from headaches and back pain to insomnia, hair loss, and heart palpitations. By contrast, those who looked back on uncomplicated, harmonious relationships were far more likely to have come to terms with their situation. Even after another two or three years, the results were much the same. Survivors of conflicted relationships more often reported a yearning for their lost spouse, while those from more loving relationships had been more successful in moving on with their lives and were more likely to report something along the lines of "I carry him within me" or "I know she'll always be there."

Another finding of the Harvard study, somewhat less surprising, was that husbands and wives who felt extremely dependent on their lost spouse had a lot more trouble adjusting to their loss. For some, the fear of going on without their lost partner was so overwhelming that they were unable to fully accept the fact that their loved one was gone. This inability to accept reality interfered with their recovery from grief and it deprived them of the energy and desire to go on with life.

The Harvard researchers concluded that the nature of the relationship between husband and wife during life is a pretty good predictor of the nature of the surviving partner's mourning. When a relationship marked by unresolved issues is ended by death, the surviving partner may replay those issues for years, perhaps for a lifetime. People yearn for their loved ones not only because they love and miss them, but also because they still have things they want to say to them, or things they still need from them, or emotions they want to express to them—and never can.

In the years since the Harvard study, we have learned a lot more about complicated grief and its causes, but the heart of the message remains unchanged: recovery from the loss of a loved one is harder if the relationship had elements of unresolved dependence, ambivalence, or conflict. Experience confirms this time and again, and it is true not only for husbands and wives, but for siblings, lovers, parents, children, friends, or just about any other close human bond. It is said that death ends a life, but it does not end a relationship.[3] The more complicated the relationship was, the more leftover conflicts, questions, and needs the mourner carries with him or her, the more likely the mourner is to remain emotionally entwined with the person who has died. This continuing attachment, as uneasy and uncomfortable in death as it was in life, interferes with the person's ability to accept and adjust to the loss. Someone stuck in this kind of emotional mire may well need help in getting out of it.

A problematic relationship is not the only reason people get stuck in the mourning process. Over the years, we have learned that mourning also can be complicated by the circumstances of a death, which can burden the mourner with traumatic memories that stand in the way of healing. The family of someone dying from cancer or Alzheimer's disease can spend months or years in a stressful world of hospitals, difficult life-and-death decisions, and sleepless nights, all the while watching someone they love tortured by illness. Death ends that trauma, only to be followed immediately by grief and the prospect of reentry into a world that may not have felt normal for a long time.

Sudden, violent death also takes a terrible toll. On an unprecedented and horrific scale, this was the case for people whose loved ones died in the attack on the World Trade Center. They watched their loved ones' deaths on television and had to bear their grief publicly and see it reflected in the eyes of the entire nation. These kinds of experiences make mourning difficult and complex, because before a person can mourn the loss of a loved one, he or she may first have to come to grips with the traumatic aftereffects of the death. In a very real sense, the experience of people who suffer the sudden, violent death of a loved one can be compared to the experience of soldiers who have been through combat. Their mourning is complicated by symptoms we associate with post-traumatic stress disorder: anxiety, undifferentiated fear, social withdrawal, and flashbacks. Their trauma can prevent them from taking even the first steps of mourning and may interfere with their capacity to feel their own grief. Rather than feeling sad or afraid, they may describe their state as "washed out" or "stunned."

These people, too, are stuck in the mourning process and will need help moving on.

Sometimes it can be difficult for someone who has experienced a loss to know whether he or she is experiencing the normal rhythms of mourning or has truly stopped making progress toward recovery. While the line isn't always obvious, I am going to introduce you to a few people who, when I met them, clearly were stuck. Each was stuck for a different reason, yet in each case, powerful feelings and painful memories had brought healing to a grinding halt. Only by recognizing and dealing with those feelings, on both a cognitive and an emotional level, were they able to come to grips with their loss and move on with their lives.

RACHAEL: Dependence and Denial

I come into the house every day and literally talk to them and tell them about my day. I imagine them talking to me. They promised me they would never leave me. I can't believe they're really gone.

WHEN SHE CAME to see me, Rachael was in her late thirties. Her parents had both died within a short span of time nearly a year before. Rachael spoke to me with pride about her career as a science teacher, the pleasure she took in her students, her fascination with nature, and how much she had always enjoyed hiking, bicycling, and other outdoor activities. She had never had a serious relationship with a man, and although she did have some good friends, the people who had always been central to her life, her best friends, were her parents. During the last few years of their lives, Rachel took care of them, tending to her father and often visiting her mother, who was then living in a nursing home. When her parents died, Rachael felt empty, without purpose or connection. She felt that in dying, her parents had taken some essential part of her with them. Rachael questioned whether she could survive without her parents and even whether life was worth living without them.

When someone we love dies, it's natural to experience a sense of unreality. In fact, that sense of unreality is one of the ways we cushion our heart against a pain that we can't absorb all at once. Sometimes we may be caught off guard. A woman may hear a particularly juicy piece of gossip, and her first impulse is to call her sister, before quickly realizing she is no longer there. Most people who lose a loved one have these thoughts now and then. It's part of the way our mind copes. There are other moments, however, when a person's *absence* is experienced. So many people describe to me an emptiness or a void that seems to rise up out of nowhere, maybe prompted by a song or a scent that reminds them of the person they have lost. Suddenly the absolute and permanent reality of death is present: I can't call my sister because she is not there and will never be there again. Some moments of recognition feel like a sudden blow; others are more subtle, producing a sadness we feel but can't name. However we take it in, the realization of death's finality is what it means to "recognize the loss," and it is always painful. When I see this pain in people who come to me for help, I know that there may not be much I can do but offer comfort. At the same time, I know that their pain signals an important passage in their healing, a final good-bye that likely will be followed by a gradual embrace of their new life.

Rachael was not ready to say good-bye. She compared losing her parents to losing a limb. And in much the same way that people who have lost a limb may report that they can still feel it, a highly dependent person may continue to feel as if, or act as if, a person who has died is still alive. While Rachael's rational self knew that her parents were dead, a part of her mind was creating phantoms, helping her to maintain the fiction that her parents were still with her. For Rachael, denial meant getting home from work on time because her parents had always expected her to be there. It meant having pretend conversations with them. To do otherwise, she said, would have felt like a betrayal. She could not bear to think of herself as someone who would abandon the two most important people in her life.

Rachael wasn't completely out of touch with reality; she knew that her parents weren't really there. Nonetheless, she kept to certain patterns in her life not because they were relevant to the life she now must lead, but because they comforted her with the illusion that her life had not changed, that her parents in some not-quite-real way were still with her. Emotionally, Rachael had been extremely dependent on her parents when they were alive. When they died, she went right on living as if they hadn't. Nearly a year after her parents' death, Rachael could not bring herself to get to the first stage of mourning: recognizing the loss.

Some people never make it past this stage. England's Queen Victoria is the quintessential example of someone who was stuck in the early phase of grief. Unable to accept the death of her beloved Albert, she engaged in a remarkable forty-year effort to keep him "alive," not only by building monuments to him, but by keeping the rituals and details of her own life and the life of her nation exactly as they were at the moment of his death . . . right down to the slippers laid out in his bedroom every evening.

While Victoria's power and resources gave her the ability to effectively make reality conform to her illusions, nobody I know has that ability today. Instead, for the most part, mourners stuck in the early stages of grief carry their phantoms within. Typically, an inability to recognize a loss takes the form of a lack of energy or apathy about forming new attachments. Sometimes it manifests itself as feelings of guilt, which may prevent a mourner from taking the necessary steps to move forward, but which he or she believes a loved one might not have wanted. Occasionally, denial collides with reality in ways that start to become apparent to friends and family, who may rightly wonder about the mourner's grip on reality. Rachael was fortunate enough to have caring friends who saw the trouble she was in and urged her to get help. Over time, she was able to identify the things in her life that had kept her tied to her parents and to reassess her life in the wake of their death. With a little help, Rachael got herself unstuck.

BARBARA: Dependence and Ambivalence

> Bob took care of everything—the house, the bills. He planned
> all our vacations, and we had wonderful adventures. He wasn't
> afraid of anything. He was a great husband and father.

BY THE TIME she came to see me, it had been four years since Barbara had lost her husband to cancer. Since that time, she had continued to work in a social service agency and had raised two teenage children. Yet she remained depressed and fearful about the future, doubting her ability to provide for her family and to make a life for herself, and continued to feel the pain of her husband Bob's death "as if it happened yesterday." She felt fatigued and had frequent headaches, and she told me that she had been feeling that way since Bob died, but that lately things were "getting worse, not better." Barbara was feeling stuck, but it wasn't immediately clear where her mourning had bogged down or why.

During her first few visits with me, Barbara talked in glowing terms about Bob. There was little doubt in my mind that they had in fact shared wonderful experiences together and that they had loved each other deeply. One day she mentioned to me that even though she considered it irrational, she could not help but feel angry toward Bob for dying and leaving her to deal with the realities of life, including an increasingly out-of-control teenage son. Despite the fact that she continually derided it as nonsensical ("That's just silly, he didn't die to get out of taking care of me and the kids"), she just couldn't let go of the feeling.

The persistence of Barbara's anger got me wondering if maybe she was leaving something out of her description of Bob and of their life together. After all, as she described it, her anger did seem irrational. Why would a woman whose husband had been dead for years, and with whom she had had a warm and loving relationship, still feel so much resentment toward him? Barbara apparently had accepted her husband's death and taken on the responsibilities of her new life, but I began to suspect that she had not come to grips with the full range of her emotions toward Bob. It was safe for Barbara to express resentment toward Bob for something that had been entirely not of his choosing, namely his illness and death. But for what else did she blame him?

Things started to move for Barbara when she began to realize that the anger she felt toward her husband was rooted in the reality of his life, not his death. In truth, Bob was a good partner in many ways, but he was not good with money and not good at sharing power in their relationship. It turned out that not all of the adventures Barbara and Bob had shared were quite so wonderful. The more we talked, the more Barbara's store of anger began to surface. Much of this anger had to do with the fact that Bob repeatedly had lost money on investments and that his financial "adventures" led to their being evicted from their home three times over a period of ten years. Much as she loved him, the evictions and constant worry about money had left Barbara with deeply conflicted feelings toward her husband. She could not move forward until she was able to recognize and express the full range of her feelings toward Bob.

You may be thinking, was it really necessary to dredge up all this old stuff? The best answer I can give you is to describe how the process worked for Barbara. As she allowed herself to take an honest look at the man she had been married to, warts and all, Barbara was able to put her life with him in perspective in a way that had a direct bearing on the way she lived her life without him. Having shed the myth of Bob as the perfect husband and provider, she came to understand that she had faced hard times before, and this realization strengthened her self-confidence and her faith in the future.

By idealizing Bob, she had minimized herself; looking at Bob more realistically helped her to see her own strengths. As a result, she very quickly began to take control of her life, getting her finances back into balance and finding help for her son. Within months she had begun to reinvest in life, becoming involved for the first time since her husband's death in a new relationship.

The anger Barbara felt when her husband died is something many people experience when they lose a loved one. It is normal to have a residue of resentment when a person dies, just as it is normal in life to experience a range of emotions toward anyone with whom you share a long-term intimate relationship. Anger, disappointment, and guilt don't just evaporate when someone dies. If these feelings—all the feelings that were present in the relation-ship—are not acknowledged and expressed, the result is often that a person becomes trapped in an emotional maze, bumping up against one invisible, impenetrable wall after another.

There are many reasons why it can be hard for people to confront all of their feelings about someone they have loved and lost. Sometimes it's a sense of loyalty, the feeling that the person did the best he or she could. Sometimes it's guilt about what we might have, should have, or could have said during a person's life. Sometimes memories of the person struggling as they approach death can get in the way of other memories—good and bad. And sometimes we hold back our feelings out of fear, because certain memories are simply so terrible, so emotion laden, that we keep them locked up and out of sight.

Anger—the anger we're aware of and the anger we try to deny—is very often the tie that binds us to someone who has died. Barbara's anger was fairly close to the surface and was tempered by a deep love and many fond memories. Not everyone is as fortunate as Barbara, whose relationship, when all was said and done, was founded on love. Some relationships—some very close, lasting, and interdependent relationships—are so dominated by the darker range of human emotions that whatever love they may once have held is too feeble a memory to offer much comfort to those who mourn. Yet people who were involved in dysfunctional relationships do mourn, particularly if they were mainly a victim in the relationship. What they often discover is that they are mourning not so much what was, but what never was and never will be. That was the case with Suzanne, the grandmother we met earlier.

SUZANNE: Anger and Love

My mother did what she wanted. She could be mean, especially when she was drinking. She smoked like a chimney, even after the doctor told her that smoking would kill her. I would yell at her to stop. It kills me to think about how I yelled at her. I just wanted so much for her to live, and I was so angry that she didn't care enough about her family to at least try.

But your mother is your mother. No matter what she is. Now when I think about her, I have to believe that she realizes that I loved her no matter what she did. I just wish I could think about her and feel some kind of acceptance, some kind of peace.

SUZANNE'S MOTHER WAS an alcoholic who spent her early married years drinking, smoking, and fighting with Suzanne's father, who also was an alcoholic. The first question that might come to your mind when hearing Suzanne's story is, why was Suzanne so upset about her mother's death? When Suzanne first came in to talk to me, she had the same question. She said that she had few memories of her childhood. She believed that she had never really known her mother, didn't understand who she was and never would. While this upset her, what really frustrated her—what she really could not understand—was why she just couldn't stop thinking about her mother. If she had never really known her mother, never felt close to her, then why couldn't she stop thinking about her? Why was she becoming more and more obsessed with thoughts of her? Suzanne was hard on herself, critical of her grief and her tears. She wanted to forget, get over it, and move on. But she could not.

Suzanne's own life could not have been more different than her mother's. She had good, loving relationships with her husband, children, and grandchildren. Her own painful childhood was not a place she wanted to revisit, and it took weeks before she was willing to talk about what she remembered of her mother. But once she began, what emerged was a steady flow of images: vivid, terrible, and true.

When children grow up in a chaotic, violent household, they often respond by going inside themselves, essentially separating from their environment. They create a kind of emotional cocoon for themselves, a place where they don't feel or think about much of anything. It is a way of surviving, and it spares them from feelings that would be too painful to bear.

When children who learn to cope by suppressing their feelings grow into adulthood and experience a parent's death, they often are unable—at least initially—to bring into conscious awareness the feelings that were buried so long ago. Not being able to identify the source of their discomfort, to experience and acknowledge their feelings, they get stuck. Suzanne believed that she never really had known or understood her mother. As she began to recall and string together snippets of memory, it became clear that Suzanne *had* known her mother, sometimes all too well.

Suzanne had never entirely forgotten certain angry scenes, but she had come to view them from a detached perspective, much as if she were watching a movie: "I didn't think about it at the time. I just lived it." Now, as she began to put herself back into those scenes, Suzanne remembered what the impact had been on her. The cruel words she recalled had been spoken not by some random stranger but by her own mother: the attacks were personal. Suzanne began to ask not only, "Why was she like that?" but "How could she have said those things to *me*?" As the full range and magnitude of Suzanne's emotions came to the surface, she began to realize that she was not just sad and frustrated. She was angry, furious with her mother for not having done better—for not trying, for Suzanne's sake, to get sober, to stop raging, and to give her the care and love she needed.

As Suzanne's memories surfaced, she also began to remember other things. She remembered moments of bittersweet tenderness with her mother, though few and far between. She remembered as well that her mother had talked to her about her own frightening stories of abuse as a child. Suzanne began to develop a more nuanced and more complete picture of who her mother really had been. The picture became, if not comforting, at least more complete.

Often, as we talked, Suzanne would question the value of bringing up things she couldn't do anything about, things that were in the past. In fact, adults who have lost a parent with whom they had a conflicted relationship often say they just want to forget the bad and remember the good. But you can't forget something until you've remembered it—really remembered it. There's a difference between burying old anger and experiencing it and letting it go. This is what Suzanne discovered in the course of mourning her mother. By depersonalizing and blocking memories of her mother's behavior, Suzanne had managed to avoid feeling much of the pain her mother had caused her, but at the expense of understanding. When her mother died, Suzanne was left with unanswered questions that simply could not be resolved without those memories. So Suzanne had been stuck. Once she found the place she was stuck, the memories—and the answers—came forward in a torrent. She now had the understanding she had been searching for and could grieve not just for the mother she had lost, but for the mother she had longed for and never had.

MARGARET: Chronic Abuse and Unrelenting Anger

> I can remember being eight and thinking that all I wanted
> to do was disappear. I would think: I'm nothing to my father
> but something to be used. But the worst part was knowing
> I wouldn't get it right and the fear that he was going to hurt
> me. That feeling is still so deep in my gut, that I'm going to
> get hurt. My sister says it's like he's still hurting us from the
> grave.

I FIRST MET Margaret six months after her brother Chris died in an
automobile accident. He was thirty-six at the time of his death, two
years younger than Margaret, and they had had what she described
as a very close and special relationship. Of her three siblings, Chris
was the one who understood and accepted her. Like her, Chris was
something of a loner; given to self-reflection, he was uncomfortable
in social situations and tended to drift through life without a real
home or a long-term partner. Survivors of a childhood marred by
chaos and abuse, Margaret and Chris were drinking buddies from
the time Chris was thirteen until they were both in their thirties.
"We went through things the same way. We felt things the same
way. We were twin flames."

Along with her grief about her brother's death, Margaret
found herself confronted by the reawakening of painful feelings
about her father, who had died sixteen years before. Margaret's
father was an alcoholic who verbally and physically abused every
member of her family. She described her relationship with him as
"a twenty-five year long ordeal." Margaret had long suspected that
her reluctance to marry and have children was the result of seeing
her parents' marriage and never wanting to take the chance of ending up like her mother, under the thumb of an irrational tyrant. For
a similar reason, Margaret had chosen to work as an independent
management consultant, work that did not require her to enter into

a long-term relationship with any one organization. For Margaret, being safe meant always being able to walk away if things became unpleasant, never being required by contract or personal indebtedness to do something she didn't want to do. Too much of her early life had been a tortured exercise in trying to please her father, doing what he told her to do, trying not to make him angry, and always hoping for some sign from him that she was not completely useless.

Even now, the memory of her many failed attempts to earn her father's love and approval were enough to unravel Margaret's composure and convince her that she could not put herself in the position of being rejected again. She would rather be alone than risk that kind of hurt. Margaret had spent years in therapy talking about her early childhood and believed her memories of those experiences had been "detoxified"—that they no longer evoked feelings of powerlessness and shame. But Chris's death had revived these feelings.

As we've seen, certain qualities in a relationship—dependence, ambivalence, anger—tend to be associated with more difficult and complicated mourning. Survivors of abuse must deal with those same complications *plus* the even more persistent and intrusive set of feelings related to the traumatic nature of their experience.

Listening to Margaret, it became clear that throughout her childhood she had experienced the terror and helplessness that are two of the defining characteristics of trauma. And though the abuse had happened many years ago, the memories of it had not lost their emotional power. Before Margaret could stop replaying old memories and come to terms with her feelings about her father, she needed to learn how to cope with strong emotions—a capacity she had not developed in childhood. She needed to be able to tune in to her emotions, recognize when old memories were threatening to overwhelm her, and find ways of coping with her feelings instead of shutting herself down emotionally. Only then could she make sense of her feelings about her father and finally escape his destructive hold on her. The energy freed from this unhealthy attachment could then be redirected toward grieving her losses—the love she had lost and the love she never had—and moving forward in her life.

NORMAN: Trauma and Transformation

> There was a time in my mother's illness when her mind went and it was like she wasn't my mother anymore. Sometimes she didn't know who I was and she would look at me with complete terror in her eyes, or it would be like she was looking right through me. I can't stop thinking about those times, and whenever I do, I feel sick.

WHEN HE CAME to see me, Norman was in his twenties. The past few years of his life had been about two things: getting his career off the ground and caring for his mother, who had gone through a prolonged illness that led to dementia and incapacity, and recently, her death.

Norman and his mother had had a close, loving relationship, and a big part of Norman's sorrow came from the loss of someone on whom he had always depended for unconditional love and support. But along with his understandable heartache, Norman was troubled by thoughts and feelings that were new to him: insecurity, anxiousness, indecision, and fears about the future. When I asked Norman to describe his feelings, he said, "I'm overwhelmed, like I'm supposed to be in charge, but I'm not. I feel like everything is out of my control."

I asked him to tell me about another time in his life when he had felt that way, and what came to mind was a series of memories, frightening memories, of his mother in various stages of emotional and physical decay. In the course of her illness, Norman's mother would go through periods when she did not know who or where she was and did not recognize her own son. These times were terrifying for Norman. On one occasion, he had run from the room as his mother crawled across the floor, trying to grab hold of his leg. The image tormented Norman, reminding him just how very ill his mother had been and leaving him with an unshakeable belief that he had abandoned his mother at her time of greatest need.

While the particulars are Norman's alone, what he went through is similar to what many people experience as their loved ones near the end of their lives. Death is mystifying and tragic. *Dying*, however, is tangible, immediate, and often frightening. People who witness their loved ones die a terrible death are often left with memories so vivid and unremitting that they can think of little else: not the person's life, not their relationship with the person and all that they shared.

Norman saw his mother consumed by illness over a period that lasted for years. He felt as though the images of his mother's dying were indelibly printed on his brain, and he feared that no amount of talking was going to get rid of them or lessen the pain he felt when he thought about them. This is the nature of traumatic memory—an image that seems to exist apart from time, with the potential to trigger old stores of emotional pain every time the image is recalled. Time does not drain these images of their power. Nothing we say to ourselves and nothing anyone else says seems to help. As we'll see, because of the way the brain stores these memories, it can feel as if they are happening *right now*.

Any death of a loved one presents us with a reality that stretches to the limit our capacity for understanding and acceptance. When the death involves prolonged suffering, witnesses to this suffering are left with emotional injuries that need attention. Likewise, when the death is violent and sudden—a car crash, a suicide, a murder—thoughts of a loved one's last moments can invade a survivor's thoughts and dreams, even if he or she did not actually witness the death.

It is said that there are very few good ways to die and a lot of bad ways. Not very many people have the good fortune to die at an advanced age, painlessly, with their faculties intact to the end and their family at the bedside. Of the many departures from this ideal, all those bad ways, some are particularly hard on the survivors.

In Norman's case, once we had identified the memories that triggered negative feelings about himself, we were able to look at how these feelings were interfering with his mourning. Norman was unable to hold on to positive memories of his mother because of his guilt about having failed as his mother's caregiver. Talking about his feelings brought some relief, but not enough. I suggested to Norman that we try EMDR, which stands for eye movement desensitization and reprocessing, a therapy that has shown promise in helping people suffering from various types of traumatic experiences.[4] EMDR is a technique by which the fragments of a traumatic experience—the thoughts, feelings, and body sensations that the person experienced during the trauma—are reactivated and then connected to internal resources and areas of strength that were not available to the person when the trauma occurred. In this way, a belief that has become attached to a particular memory—in Norman's case, "I failed my mother" or "I was not a good son"— can be modified. For example, Norman remembered times during his mother's illness when his mother had told him just how much she appreciated all of Norman's love and sacrifice. Norman came to understand that while there may have been times when his fears got the better of him, his mother had in fact felt Norman's loving presence right up to the end. By integrating this new understanding of events into his narrative of the past, Norman was able to embrace his memories of his mother and get past the stuck point in his mourning.

Techniques like those I used with Norman are a way of helping people not only *think* about their experiences and themselves in a different way, but to actually *feel* different. There are many such techniques, and not all entail intensive work with a therapist. I'll talk more about EMDR and other approaches to grief and trauma in the chapters ahead.

Getting Unstuck

WHATEVER STRUGGLES EXIST between two people in life, when one of them dies it falls to the survivor to resolve them. When a relationship is relatively loving and uncomplicated, the thoughts and emotions that constitute mourning will flow freely. In time, understanding and acceptance will follow and mourning will cease to be the emotional center of the survivor's life. The pattern is altogether different, however, when thoughts and feelings cannot flow easily, when they are too painful, confusing, or frightening to deal with. When that happens, mourning breaks down. People get stuck.

Each of the people you have just met, and those whose stories you will read in the pages that follow, were stuck. Each lived through losses from which they believed they could not recover. But they *did* recover. All were able to discover why they were not healing, to draw what they needed from the past, and to find a path back to the life that was waiting for them. Along the way, many gained a better understanding not only of what they had lost, but of what they still might create for themselves in the years ahead.

CHAPTER 2

When You Need Someone
Too Much to Let Go

*People, people who need people, are the luckiest
people in the world.*
—Bob Merrill, "People"

*W*ell, yes—and sometimes no. To love and
depend on other people, and have them love and
depend on us, can be the most fulfilling part of life.
Our connections with other people can be a source of comfort,
support, and security. We may depend on a spouse to share the hard
work and many pleasures of raising a family, or on a parent to be
there with words of encouragement when we're feeling down. It's
a rare and, I think most would agree, lonely individual who goes
through life not needing and depending on anyone.

But too much dependence on someone else can be an impedi-
ment to growth and can keep people from recognizing their own
abilities and strengths. Overdependence provides a ready excuse
for avoiding potentially difficult engagement in one's own life: a
man who says no to every social invitation from potential friends
because he "must get home" to his mother, a wife who defers to

her husband on all important decisions because "he knows so much more" about how to manage their lives than she does.

Sometimes a person's degree of dependence on someone else does not become apparent until that person dies. Then the mourner must face the most painful loss of his or her life without the one person who provided the greatest source of support.

When we lose someone we love, life changes in many ways, from the most mundane to the most profound. The person who cooked dinner for us, paid the bills, or changed the oil in the car is no longer there. We have to find other people to do these things for us, or we have to learn to do them ourselves. On the more significant side of the ledger are those changes that cannot be simply or easily accommodated. The loss of a spouse's love and support; a parent's understanding and comfort; a brother's friendship: there are things that each of us depends on another person to provide, many of them unique to the relationship. There is no getting around the fact that when someone who is a big part of our lives dies, we lose not only the person, but so many things large and small that made us feel safe and connected in the world.

The death of someone we love isn't something to "get over" as much as it is a reality to which we slowly adjust. Little by little, people accommodate to changed circumstances and do what they can to fill the void left by the person who is no longer there. There may be no one else to do the cooking, but people can learn to cook. People also learn to live with the more significant kinds of loss and change brought about by death. The person who has been lost can never be replaced, but there is love and connection to be found in the world, and people who have found these things once, often find them again.

While that fact is of little comfort to someone who has just lost a loved one, in time most mourners are able to believe in a future in which their pain will have eased and their hearts will again be open to love. Most people also believe deep down that as hard as it may be for them to go on with their lives, they can do it. Some speak of going on with life because "that's what Mom would have wanted" or because "living a happy and meaningful life is the best way for me to honor my husband's memory."

But for people who were overly dependent on someone who has died, the feeling may persist of being lost without their loved one—so lost that they fear they may never find comfort or refuge again.

What Is Excessive Dependence?

So people who need people, or at least people who need a particular person too much, arguably are not so lucky, especially when that particular person dies. Yet such relationships are hardly a rarity, and most of us have probably had the experience, at least once in our lives, of feeling that a certain person is absolutely essential to our existence.

The question that arises then is what is "excessive" dependence? In simplest terms, it's a degree of reliance on another person (or people) that makes it hard for someone to believe they can exist on their own. Someone who is in an overly dependent relationship feels compelled, regardless of the degree of damage to themselves or their sense of self-worth, to seek approval from another person in order to ensure their continued safety and sense of self-worth.[1]

Dependency tends to compromise a person's ability to complete the first task of all mourners, which is to acknowledge that the death has occurred.[2] If the level of someone's dependence on another person is extreme, confronting the reality that they are no longer available is understandably likely to be very difficult.

Dependent relationships serve a purpose, and often that purpose is emotional and even physical security: to provide a place of refuge from the real and imagined threats of the wider world. Take that relationship away through death, and the survivor suddenly feels exposed, vulnerable to whatever the world may have in store. People in this situation often say to me that they simply "cannot imagine life" without their loved one. While for some this is an expression of how sad and lonely they feel, for others it is a simple, straightforward truth. So wrapped up was their identity with the person who died that they can no longer conceive of themselves, if they ever could, as being an independent person capable of building an independent life. They have no image in their mind of what life will be like for the next day or week, much less in future months and years.

People in this situation get stuck in a kind of suspended state, unable to make changes in their lives, even changes that at some level they need or want to make. Sometimes it's self-doubt that stops them, sometimes it's a gnawing sense that what they're planning would not be something of which the deceased would approve:

> My mother died a year and a half ago. She had the bigger of
> the bedrooms, and I'd like to move into it, but my dog sleeps
> with me, and she never wanted a dog in that room.

The signal characteristic of people who are stuck in grief because of their overdependence on someone who has died is an underlying rumbling of panic, a barely suppressed fear of being unable to function on their own. For people in this situation, it's as if all the oxygen suddenly has been sucked from their environment. How can they possibly survive?

The connection between dependency in life and difficulty in recovery from grief is intuitive; the more dependent a person is on someone else, the harder it is for that person to believe that he or she can have a life when that person dies. Add to this the fact that such people may be reluctant to admit the extent of their dependency, even to themselves, and it becomes apparent why the mourning process can break down.

For people in highly dependent relationships, the relationship and their understanding of it tend to dominate their self-identity. Any questioning of the relationship, especially after the person with whom they shared it has died, gets pretty quickly into very sensitive emotional territory. In years of talking to people who have lost love ones, I've yet to come across anyone who embraced with enthusiasm my suggestion that their relationship may have been overly dependent. Rather, they are likely to be put off by what they believe such a suggestion might imply about them, or about the person who has died. So before going on, let's put some myths about dependency to rest.

First of all, being in a dependent relationship does not mean a person is weak. I meet many women whose husbands earned most of the money and made most of the decisions about how to spend it. Control over finances may have extended to control over how and where the couple lived, where they vacationed, whom they saw socially, and so on. It's not surprising that many women in this situation feel trepidation about their ability to manage alone. Yet the overwhelming majority do move on to build a full life for themselves without their spouse. Moreover, most along the way discover strengths and abilities they did not know they had, or perhaps had not felt free to display when their spouses were alive.

Whatever the underlying reason for their dependence, women and men who are new to the experience of life outside the framework of a dependent relationship often come to realize that they can in fact depend on *themselves* to a much greater extent than they ever imagined. The discovery of their own strength doesn't take away their grief, doesn't make them less sad or lonely. But it can ease their fear, which frees them to imagine the possibilities of a new life.

A second point that's important to understand is that just because a relationship is overdependent does not mean that it isn't based on love. Every close relationship is built on a complex emotional base of needs and motivations. Sometimes people's own needs—for company, for attention, or for control—override the knowledge of how they should behave if they have someone else's best interests at heart, even someone they love dearly.

An aging father may know at some level that he should encourage his caretaker daughter to get out more, but he may not be able to face the time without her. A husband may realize that keeping his wife in the dark about their finances could leave her vulnerable in the event of his death, but he may be afraid that in sharing the information he may appear weak or as a poor provider. Parents may discourage an adult child from taking a job or pursuing a relationship that might threaten their own access to his or her time.

People do these sorts of things all the time, sometimes consciously, sometimes unconsciously. It doesn't necessarily make them selfish or uncaring people. It doesn't mean they don't love the people whom they treat less-than-fairly. They may even believe they are shielding him or her from unnecessary worry or struggle. Nevertheless, even the loving intention to protect another person from the world, to relieve someone of the responsibility of having to earn a living (she might fail), to form relationships (she might get hurt), or to become an adult (it's a cold, cruel world out there) is ultimately to do a disservice, because it deprives the person of the opportunity to develop into an independent, capable human being.

So, in speaking of overdependency, the purpose is not to impose a disparaging label, or to say that someone is weak, or that someone was bad or unloving; it is simply to acknowledge that some relationships, even relationships with people who loved us and whom we loved, leave us ill prepared to face life when that person dies.

Sometimes dependent relationships work well enough. While some are destructive and conflicted, many are not. Often people are content to make the tradeoffs involved in dependency, whether implicitly or explicitly. After a death, however, whatever comfort and security was provided by the relationship suddenly is gone, and the consequences of dependency can become all too apparent. Unable to move back, afraid to move forward, overdependent people can very easily become stuck in their grief.

Here are the stories of some people whose mourning was complicated by overdependency and who ultimately found the strength to move on and rebuild their lives.

LISA

Like so many of the stories people tell me, Lisa's was first and foremost a love story. After meeting and falling in love with Al while in her thirties, Lisa willingly gave up a single life she had considered somewhat dull and entered a married life defined by Al's ambitious goals and interests. Two years after he died, Lisa felt her life had stalled. She still grieved. She was afraid to make critical decisions about how and where she should live. She needed help in identifying the parts of life with her husband that she wanted to retain and the parts that no longer made sense for her. And she needed assurance that she was able and entitled to shape her own future.

Lisa had been married to Al for sixteen years when he died. Their time together had been adventurous and romantic. Al was an avid sailor and had founded a successful restaurant. They spent the first nine years of their marriage on Al's sailboat, traveling the world together. When she came to see me, Lisa was grieving her husband and missing him terribly. But what made her grief particularly hard to bear was the feeling of having lost her entire *life*. The boat and the restaurant were Al's passions, and she had found pleasure in sharing them with *him*. Now that he was gone, she continued to go through the motions of the life he had created for them, but she was deeply unhappy. She knew she had to find her own way and her own interests, but she was uncertain of her abilities and had convinced herself that to make the attempt would be to abandon Al and all he had meant to her.

The restaurant in particular was a source of worry and guilt for Lisa. Al had built it into a neighborhood landmark, with a loyal customer base and long-term employees who had come to think of it as a second home. She felt an obligation to keep the restaurant going because "that's what Al would have wanted." Friends encouraged her to keep the restaurant, and Lisa was afraid that if she sold it, they would regard her as weak and as a failure.

But Lisa didn't seem weak to me. In fact, she seemed tough and smart. In addition to running the restaurant—which was as successful under her management as it had been under Al's—Lisa had a full-time career working as a counselor in a substance abuse center. She also was a recovered alcoholic, with twenty years of hard-won sobriety to her credit. Lisa's own struggle with alcohol, and her determination not to "fall into that hole again," was a big part of why she no longer wanted to be involved with the restaurant. Not only was it extremely stressful holding down two jobs, but one of those jobs involved being around alcohol and people drinking it. Lisa knew addiction, in theory and firsthand. She understood that the restaurant—Al's restaurant—with all the emotions it evoked, and the ready availability of alcohol, was the worst possible environment for her, and that being there put her sobriety and everything it meant at risk. She understood this, but just couldn't get past the need to do what she believed Al would have wanted her to do:

> The energy of the restaurant pulls me in, and I feel my life becoming smaller and smaller. It's like when Al and I first set out on the big trip . . . I feel isolated and scared. But I know the restaurant was everything to him, and he would have wanted me to keep it going.

By no means is it unusual, of course, for a surviving spouse to think about what her husband would want her to do and the decisions he would advise her to make. Many people find that being able to tap into the perspective and wisdom of a lost loved one provides reassurance and consolation.[3] But for Lisa, the desire to follow Al's imagined wishes made it impossible for her to move forward, even though the prospect of staying where she was made her feel sad and lonely. Lisa told me once that in the years they were at sea, "interdependence was a matter of survival." But she knew things were different now: to survive, and thrive, she would have to find a way to strike out on her own.

For Lisa, or anyone in her situation, it can be comforting to hold on to elements of a life once shared with a loved one who has died. But hold on too tightly, and the process of healing from loss can grind to a halt. Before a person can begin to heal, it is necessary to accept at some level that death has fundamentally altered his or her life. This can be hard for two reasons: it means facing the fact of irreversible loss, and it means coming to grips with the reality of having to rebuild a new life. Confronted with the death of someone they love, people like Lisa can feel honor bound to do what that person "would have done." The sad truth, however, is that none of us can re-create a life that centered on the presence of a person who is no longer alive to share it.

While there can be continuity of sorts after someone has died, death draws a sharp boundary between what was and what is. Acceptance of this fact does not mean forgetting, abandoning, or replacing a loved one. But it does mean distinguishing between the relationship that existed before, along with all its obligations and commitments, and the relationship that exists now. It means facing life without the living presence of the person who has died. As we'll see, Lisa was able to adjust to the realities of her new life and ultimately to feel a sense of excitement about her future and pride in her ability to shape it. What Lisa came to realize was that as much as she missed Al and some parts of her life with him, she was capable of being on her own and even enjoying her independence. Gradually, Lisa's sadness became less of a constant companion, and her energy and pleasure in life were reignited. For someone like Lisa, taking a realistic look at her past and present life went a long way toward helping her find the confidence she needed to move forward. For some people, however, dependency is so deeply ingrained in their sense of self, that getting unstuck from grief isn't as straightforward as it was for Lisa. Some people have grown into adulthood with a distinct tendency toward being dependent on others and a deeply held resistance to the idea that they can function on their own. That's how it was for Barbara.

BARBARA

Barbara, whom we met briefly in Chapter 1, came to see me five years after the death of her husband, Bob. She spent much of our initial time together alternately weeping and railing against her husband for having left her. The degree of Barbara's distress seemed out of proportion to the reality of her situation: she had a job that paid the bills, she was able to support herself and her two children, and she had a house and some money in the bank. Yet, despite all evidence to the contrary, Barbara felt as though her life was on the verge of spinning out of control. She spoke of a desperate yearning to have someone rescue her. Whatever she looked like on the outside, Barbara let me know that on the inside she felt like a little girl who was incapable of taking care of herself, let alone her family. The more I heard from that little girl, the more I understood why she felt so angry and scared.

Like many girls, Barbara was raised by parents who adored her, but whose continuing affection required certain sacrifices on Barbara's part. She was the perfect "china doll": fair-skinned, delicate, sweet. She knew how to make her parents happy and was eager to do so. Unlike her sister, who often rebelled and paid a price for it, Barbara tried to anticipate what her parents wanted of her before they asked. She assumed a caretaking role toward them early, and it was a source of pride to her that she was the family peacemaker and confidant.

What stood out for Barbara about her girlhood was what she had learned about the importance of being "pleasing"—pleasing to the eye and pleasing in her behavior. She was taught to be quiet, attentive to others, and cheerful. She learned through experience that acting pleasing was the surest way to win her parents' approval. And she was told repeatedly by them that this same behavior one day would ensure the attention and affection of a man who would take good care of her. The importance of attracting such a man was never in question. It simply was assumed that Barbara could not provide for herself or make decisions for herself. If she ever gave evidence that she was not fully with the program—if she objected to something her father or mother said, if she expressed an independent thought or intention—their disapproval was swift. It was hard for her to say what had hurt more, the harsh words of disapproval or her mother's warning that if she kept it up no man would ever want her.

So, despite five years of successful independence, Barbara remained convinced that she needed a man to take care of her. The ingrained belief that she was helpless on her own provided a steady source of anger and resentment toward her absent husband. Fear and rage poured out of Barbara. She was the very picture of someone refusing to budge from a position of chronic mourning.[4] But at the same time, inside, Barbara was outgrowing her old self.

As Barbara filled in the details of her marriage, it became clear that her husband had not exactly been the perfect provider. In fact, he continually overreached, and more than once, unable to keep up with the payments on their home, they had had to move. The more she revealed about Bob's flaws as a husband and provider, the more angry and frustrated Barbara became. Relying on Bob had never really worked out well for Barbara, but she had believed in the myth that he was her protector; it would take a while for her to believe she could manage without him, and it also would take time for her to accept that he was not the man she had believed him to be. Barbara needed to disentangle herself from her dependence on Bob, but that was easier said than done: "I feel like he's permeated me. I almost feel like I need an exorcism."

Barbara no longer could remain the woman she had been in her marriage—dependent, passive, infinitely adaptable to other people's needs, wants, and failures. She was changing, and she had mixed feelings about it. She was tired of waiting for someone to "save" her and wasn't sure anymore that she even wanted to get married again. Still, she couldn't shake the view of herself as a helpless child.

The Roots of Dependency

BARBARA IS FAR from alone in her feelings. Many people, mostly women but many men as well, have a deeply ingrained propensity toward dependence. Their stories differ, but there are common threads that often go back to their very earliest relationships.

A lot of the most thoughtful work on this topic has been done by people who have an interest in what is called *attachment theory*. Simply put, attachment theory recognizes that people are born with an innate tendency to become attached to and dependent on whoever takes care of them, and that early attachments tend to shape relationships later in life.

By and large, children who receive consistent and unconditional love from an adult, usually their mother, grow up confident in themselves and confident that love will always be available to them. As they mature, they tend to form new, mutually rewarding relationships that mirror the first—loving and neither requiring nor expecting that love will come only at a price to their own self-fulfillment.

Children who are deprived of that early support, however, tend to form relationships of a different type. When love from a parent is sometimes there and sometimes not, children learn to do whatever it takes to hang on. This is what Barbara learned to do; playing the china doll was what seemed to ensure her parents' love, so she acted the part. As an adult, she continued to believe that being a dependent and pliable little girl was the way to get love, even as this image no longer matched the woman she was or needed to be.

To a friend or even a casual acquaintance, nothing could be more obvious than the fact that Barbara was a successful woman who had every reason to step confidently into her new life. But from Barbara's perspective, the fact of her own independence was a sure sign that she was a *failure*. Barbara had learned from her parents that her primary mission in life was to be pleasing to them and to a future husband. According to her parents' definition, a pleasing woman didn't make her own decisions, didn't assert herself, and didn't manage her own money. So here she was, a successful woman who saw herself as a failure and who was convinced that the very qualities that had brought her success—her intelligence, will, and capacity for independent action—would guarantee only more failure in the future. No wonder she was scared, angry, and resentful. While Barbara had in fact moved on with her life in the ways that she needed to in order to support herself and her family, emotionally she had not moved on at all. She was stuck, and very afraid, in an unhappy, lonely place.

Barbara's experience, while unique in its particulars, is not unusual. In the Harvard study mentioned in the last chapter, mourners who had early life experiences of insecure attachments remained uninterested in their work or in seeing people years after their spouse had died. They were reluctant to make changes in their lives or decisions about their future. They spoke of feeling increasingly isolated and depressed. Fearful of being unable to function on their own, they simply refused to move forward.

There are no universal truths here. Not everyone who grows up with an insecure attachment to his or her mother becomes dependent later in life. Countless other influences—other relationships, other experiences—can offset or override the formative impact of early attachment. This being said, attachment theory can help us understand why some people seem to have a particular vulnerability to certain kinds of relationships and certain reactions to loss. When someone comes in for help five years after the death of her husband, still actively grieving and still frightened and unsure of her ability to survive without him, I'm interested in knowing about the relationship, of course. But I also want to know about how she grew up and what she was taught about her strengths and her ability to take care of herself.

Dependence and Denial

WHENEVER I RUN a group for adults who have lost a parent or a spouse, I ask people to bring in pictures, letters, anything that they want to share with the group. I do this because it evokes memories, because it brings the presence of lost loved ones into the room even more vividly, and because it helps bring them to the very first step of mourning: acknowledgment of the reality that they have suffered an irreversible loss. We pass the pictures around: this is my father dancing at my wedding; this is my husband before he got sick; this is my mother cooking dinner; this is my mother just before she died.

Almost always there is at least one person who announces that she couldn't possibly bring in pictures because she can't bear to see anything that reminds her of her mother—her clothes, her furniture, her favorite flower. All of it evokes unbearable waves of grief.

At this point, someone else in the group may interject that he has the opposite problem—he can't *stop* looking at pictures. He has not been able to put away any of his loved one's clothes or even to take her medicine out of the medicine cabinet.

In effect, these mourners are using opposite strategies to achieve the same objective: protection from a very painful reality. Whether by shielding themselves from any reminder of the person who died or by keeping everything as it was before the death, each is trying to manage the dose of grief so that it is not more than he or she believes is bearable.

For just about anyone who experiences the loss of a loved one, it takes time for the reality of death to sink in. It's not unusual to hear, "I wake up every day and think I'll call her" or "I see something in the store and I'll think, 'he'd like that, I'll get it for him.'" Taking in the reality of loss is something that happens little by little, through the accumulated experience, day after day, of life without the person who has died.

And I often think that's how it needs to happen—that we have a kind of emotional thermostat that keeps us from taking in more than we can handle, a built-in mechanism that protects us from being overloaded by painful information. That explains why mourning is not a linear process. Contrary to what they may expect or even hope for, most people do not feel very bad in the beginning and better with each passing day. Instead, people tend to experience "waves" of grief, to shift back and forth between looking back and looking ahead, between immersion in sadness and periods of distance from their grief. People find that they unexpectedly experience a "good" day, when they're feeling like their old self. They go to work, take care of the kids, and make social arrangements. The next day they may be unable to bring themselves to get out of bed in the morning.[5] It may feel odd, but it's normal and necessary to travel back and forth between these two emotional landscapes for an extended period after a loss. Being able to look back and fully grieve and being able to look ahead to a new life are both essential parts of mourning. And to do either, it is necessary to take the first step in mourning, to get past denial and to accept that a death has happened and that life from now on will be fundamentally different than before.

For someone who was in a dependent relationship, getting past denial may be the most difficult task of mourning. Acknowledging that the person has died means confronting a perceived reality of being utterly alone and unprepared for whatever may come next. Having lost the person who made all of the decisions, the mourner now has no idea how to manage his or her own life. Having lost the person whose approval sustained a sense of self-worth, the mourner now feels empty and unmoored. Too bereft to look back, and too frightened to look ahead, the mourner simply gets stuck, sometimes for years, in the same place that others pass through relatively quickly after a death.

Like all psychological defenses, denial is useful up to a point, and then it becomes a problem. Lisa kept on running the restaurant just as if Al were still alive, and for a time that gave her a certain comfort that she was doing what he would have wanted. Barbara continued to think of herself as someone who was taken care of by someone else because she always *had* been taken care of by someone else. To an extent, both carried on for years in ways that suggested their loved one was still present and that death had not irrevocably changed their lives. For some time after their losses, these mental fictions helped them cope, but when the contradictions between their perceptions and reality became too great, they found themselves in crisis.

Sometimes, denial of death manifests itself literally. Queen Victoria's prolonged grief and denial were so extreme that eventually it caused many in England to openly question her sanity. Rachael, the science teacher we met in the last chapter, is more typical of how the mix of denial and dependency can cause a perfectly healthy person to begin to question her own grip on reality.

RACHAEL

In several respects, Rachael was like many men and women I see who have lost a parent. She described an intensely close, positive relationship. Her parents regularly told her that she was their whole world, and she felt the same about them. Rachael described her life since her parents' death two years earlier as a kind of nightmare from which she could not shake herself awake. More than two years after their death, Rachael said, "I can't bring myself to talk about them in the past tense."

While she knew rationally that they were gone, her parents continued to be the emotional center of Rachael's life, just as they had been before their deaths. She liked to "pretend they're sitting on the couch" and would have regular conversations with them. At first, she said, conversing with them would make her feel better, but now she was beginning to wonder if "maybe it isn't so good for me to talk to them so much," though she was quick to add, "I can't turn my back on them."

It's not unusual for people to talk to a deceased loved one, and many people find it comforting to continue their relationship in this way. Two years after her parents' deaths, however, Rachael had come to a point where it was no longer comforting, and truthfully it was starting to scare her a little. Part of her wanted to stop, but another part told her she couldn't.

The roots of Rachael's emotional dependence on her parents became clear as she began to talk more about her childhood. While she continued to lament that "no one will ever love me the way my parents did," she started to express some misgivings about how she had been raised, and it became clear that her parents' love and affection had come with a price. "If I said, 'I'd like to cook something,' my mother would try to take over every single bit of the cooking." According to Rachael, her parents had tried to micromanage every aspect of her life and had reacted very harshly to any hint that she was growing and becoming independent. Her father was very supportive when she went along with his wishes but could be harsh when she refused to take his "advice." To Rachael's parents, the world was full of potential dangers. Even as an adult, it was not easy for Rachael to ignore the echo of their many warnings. "I was a nervous, fearful child, and I guess I got a good dose of that from my parents."

Not surprisingly, Rachael's decision at age thirty to move into the world beyond her parents' door was not well received by them. When she announced that she was getting her own apartment, Rachael was told by her father that he took "a dim view" of her plan: "A girl should stay home until she gets married." After she left, her mother would call to tell her that her father was sitting by the window, "waiting for you to come home." Referring to a Jewish tradition of mourning, Rachael said, "They were sitting shiva for me."[6] Rachael's mother spent the last three years of her life in a nursing home with "terrible dementia," and at this point Rachael became her father's caretaker:

> It was torture for me to visit Mom several times a week, but I
> did it. Dad remained in their home, but his heart was broken
> by the loss of Mom's companionship, and his despair pervaded
> our relationship.

It wasn't easy for Rachael to acknowledge that her parents, who had been such a loving presence and who had been so helpless and sick at the end of their lives, had deeply hurt her. If I pushed too hard, she would insist that she did not want to talk any more about negative feelings toward her parents: "Why? So I can love them less?"

After one such difficult session, I wasn't quite sure what to expect at our next meeting—or even whether there would be a next meeting—and was surprised when Rachael came in the following week and picked up right where we had left off the week before. "Last time was very painful. For a while afterward I felt that by making me remember the hurt you were taking my parents away from me, that somehow I had lost the last vestiges of them. But after a few days I started to feel better. I started to say to myself: you know, something has to change. When I think about letting go of my parents, I can't pretend it isn't frightening. It gives me a feeling of emptiness. But I see the value of moving past what I fear, and I will go forward."

Some truths are harder to accept than others. Hardest of all are the truths that violate some basic belief about ourselves and our world. For Rachael, it was the belief that her parents would always be there for her—had to be there for her—because she was not meant to be on her own. The belief was so powerful that she re-created her parents every night when she came home from work, talked to them, kept them a part of her life.

There is no absolute timeline for "normal" grieving. There is no best time to put away the clothes that will no longer be worn, any more than there is a best time to give up one's identity as someone's wife or husband, daughter or son. Nobody rushes toward the acceptance of a loved one's death—we are nudged, pushed, dragged toward acceptance by the persistent intrusion of reality, by the hundreds and thousands of moments carrying the same message of absence.

Only by remaining open to these reminders are we eventually able to comprehend, not just intellectually, but emotionally, that someone to whom we were intimately connected has died. This means being open to our senses and to our feelings and open to living life as it is and will be. Slowly, in doses, we take in reality, hold it off, and take it in again. Eventually, the very fact of continued survival contradicts the fear that a mourner cannot survive on his or her own. For those in overdependent relationships, this realization is the critical step not only in accepting death and loss, but in discovering the need, and the ability, to forge a new identity and discover a new path.

Creating a New Identity

LIKE ANYONE WHO is undertaking a difficult and frightening journey, someone who is unable to move toward acknowledging a loss needs support and reassurance, recognition of his or her suffering, and steady affirmation of his or her inner strength and ability to heal. As human beings, we are vulnerable to all kinds of physical and emotional injuries: we fall down, we crash our cars. We heal from these injuries because that is what we are built to do. Whatever care we take—bandages, splints, antibiotics—the healing itself is something that just happens. To be sure, losing a loved one is not the same as breaking a leg. But when you're weak and afraid, when it seems like nothing you or anyone else does can ever make a difference in how you feel, it may help to remember that with or without any thoughtful, brave effort on your part, *healing happens*. In fact, it takes a lot more mental energy to prevent healing—to deny the evidence all around you that your life has changed—than it does to surrender to the reality of what has happened and allow healing to occur. While it may not feel like it, in the end we're not talking about *whether* you're going to survive—you will—but *how you are going to live*.

LISA: SETTING A NEW COURSE

By now you know that Lisa loved her husband very much and loved the life they had created together. Much of Lisa's identity was defined in relationship to Al: she was his wife, his sailing partner, stepmother to his children and grandmother to their children. No wonder it seemed easier to go on with life as it had been: all the pieces were in place—except one.

A few months after I met Lisa she told me about a dream she'd had about being at a banquet. She entered a festively decorated room with lavish flowers and table settings, and everyone was beautifully dressed. She realized that it was *her* party—everyone there had come at her invitation. She took her place at the table, only to realize that there was no food! Lisa alternately grimaced and laughed as she explained that this was how she felt about her life: it was a banquet with no food. Everything looked good, everything seemed to be set, but the most important part was missing. In the midst of plenty, Lisa felt empty and sad.

Lisa decided right there that if life feels like a banquet with no food, maybe it's time to "go out and get some food!" Lisa knew she had to redefine herself and her life, to stop feeling bad about not having what she needed to be happy, and to begin thinking about how to fill the void left by Al's death.

So Lisa began to think about what would make her happy. She loved to travel and had friends in distant places whom she hadn't seen since Al's illness. She loved to garden. She dreamed of simply having some time for herself, to read, to think. She had become interested in meditation and thought she might enjoy a weekend retreat. When she thought about doing these things, Lisa felt excited, and she knew that she had to make some changes in her life to make room for them.

Longing is a powerful message that we need to be open to receiving. When the person who has been at the center of someone's life is gone, it is inevitable that he or she will experience a period of longing, of wanting nothing but the return of that person and the life they shared. But when a new longing takes hold, a longing for new ways to be in the world, new sources of nourishment, this new longing must also be given its due.

As Lisa came to understand, this was in fact exactly what Al would have wanted for her. More than anyone she had ever known,

Al was all about adventure: he wasn't afraid of the unknown, and on the contrary, relished going where he had never been. He was the last person who would want Lisa to make her life a monument to him, to keep retracing the steps they had taken together. As she began to think about herself and her commitment to Al in this way, Lisa realized that the way to honor Al's memory would be to live not *the life* he had lived, but to live *the way* he had lived: looking for the joy in life and heading straight for it.

> At first, with Al not there, I felt like 'It's not my world any-more.' Now I feel like my life can proceed, and that some of that feeling comes from Al, that he infused me with the confidence to know that you have to listen to what you feel inside, to know what you want—and then live it—that's the gift he gave me.

Lisa was grateful to her husband for this gift and wanted to live up to it. At the same time, her sense of gratitude made Lisa feel that she did not want to move on with her life if it meant forgetting who he was and what he meant to her.

Lisa decided to sell the restaurant, but first to hold a celebration there to remember Al and to say good-bye. She used part of the money from the sale of the restaurant to establish a memorial trophy at the sailing club that had been such a big part of Al's life. Having recognized that there were some broken threads in her relationships with her stepchildren, Lisa made the decision to work on repairing them, knowing that this would have been important to Al.

Then she turned to thinking about her own life. Although she was unsure about *how* she was going to go on without Al, she knew for sure that she *could* go on. Lisa had faced adversity before. Deep down she expected life to be difficult, expected to face obstacles and to have to rely on her own intelligence and courage to overcome them. In this sense, Lisa did not need to come to an entirely new understanding of herself in order to move on. But for many people, Barbara among them, rethinking who they are and want to be is an essential part of healing.

BARBARA: DEFINING A NEW SELF

Out of necessity, Barbara had redefined herself after her husband's death, but she wasn't particularly satisfied with the identity she had created. She talked about playing the "widow card"—filling out applications for her daughter's college loans and feeling uncomfortable, even contemptuous, referring to the "recent loss of my husband" when her husband had died more than five years earlier. "I don't really buy my own argument. Sure, I'm a single parent, but I've been a single parent for years. I make myself out to be needier than I am, weaker. It's like I'm not ready to let go of that identity. But I'm getting tired of thinking of myself as a victim." Barbara felt locked into the role of a dependent, a role that had been comfortable, if limiting, in her marriage to Bob. Her role in the marriage had confirmed what her parents had always told her about herself: she needed someone to take care of her. Now she was faced with having to take on responsibility for herself and her children. Like an adolescent on the verge of independence, Barbara was eager to break out and simultaneously overwhelmed by the prospect.

Barbara needed to first gain an appreciation for her strengths, and it was not hard for her to see that these were considerable. She had worked throughout her marriage and since her husband's death, had raised two teenagers and cared for her aging mother. She was a well-regarded professional whose clients looked to her for support and guidance. She had dealt with a number of crises involving her son and had begun looking at educational alternatives for him while also helping her daughter deal with the pressures of getting into college.

As she became more aware of her strengths, the idea of a future that she could create for herself became less of an impossible dream and more of an exciting possibility. The part of Barbara that was a self-reliant adult became more and more of a presence at our meetings and more a part of how Barbara saw herself. Over time, the dependent little girl emerged less and less. The person she was becoming didn't need to have a man to take care of her, but she looked forward to sharing her life with someone who "would let me fly." If living without the income of a man meant she had to sell her house, she would do it. "Bob's voice," the voice that told her she should keep the house and everything in it because "we made it together," was no longer the loudest voice in her head. More and more the voice she heard was her own, urging her forward, encouraging her to take a chance on herself, to launch herself into the world.

After a year of weekly meetings, Barbara had succeeded in getting her son placed in a special residential program, something "Bob never would have accepted" but that she had come to believe "saved my son's life." She spoke of the experience as "very empowering: This was my doing. I could get this done for my child." Barbara became involved in a relationship in which she was determined "not to hold back, to make myself smaller than I am." Most exciting for Barbara, she had attached her practice to a medical office, which provided her with a steady stream of new clients as well as a more structured work environment.

As she built a new life for herself, Barbara ultimately was able to take a more balanced view of her husband: "Bob was not a deity, and he wasn't an ogre—I've been able to realize that. It's nice to know that whoever he was, and whatever happens, I can get on with my life." Even more important than Barbara's reassessment of Bob was her new appreciation of *herself*: "I feel like I'm being reborn. I'm not afraid anymore. I thank God every day. I still have some anxiety, but after five years I feel like I've picked up the reins of my life."

RACHAEL: SLOWLY COMING TO GRIPS

As she herself had begun to suspect, Rachael's active dialogue with her parents, and her continued deference two years after their death, was beyond what most people experience. Her compliance with her parents' imagined wishes was preventing her from stepping out into a life she both wanted and feared.

Because of their tremendous influence over her life, it was very difficult for Rachael to acknowledge that her parents had hurt her, had undermined her self-confidence and her ability to live independently. Her determination to view them in a positive light is something often seen in children, who would rather see themselves as bad than believe that a parent who mistreats them is bad. People want to believe in the essential goodness of the people they need most, and Rachael was no exception.

Rachael's determinedly positive image of her parents and her low estimation of herself were intimately connected. Rachael in fact had a lot going for her—a career, interests, friends—but she couldn't begin to think about her own independence and potential without feeling that she was in some way betraying her parents.

Shortly after her realization that "something has to change," Rachael decided to take a trip to visit a friend in Texas, "someone like me, a very sensitive woman." It gave her confidence, she enjoyed it, and a few weeks later she decided to take another trip. Here's an excerpt from a letter I received from her:

> At the start of the summer, I asked God to guide me so I could get better by 30 percent (I didn't want to be presumptuous). I'm planning on going to Block Island and doing some mineral collecting in Maine. . . . I walk, swim, or bike four times a week, my deck plants are gorgeous, and people other than my parents are beginning to feel OK in my life. "Chez Rachael" is once more open for dinner parties.

When I saw her that fall, Rachael was deep into the process of rewriting the narrative of her life. The image of a passive, dependent child was being displaced by a sensitive and unconventional adult. What she had earlier described as her "social awkwardness" she now saw in a more positive light: "So I don't feel comfortable making small talk, well maybe I'm just a little bit of a maverick, a little intense . . . so be it. I have my friends, my interests, my work. I have the ability to do good in the world, to teach my students, to make people's lives better. That's what I want to focus on."

Rachael still says hello to her parents when she comes in the door after work, still tells them when something exciting is happening in her life, and asks them to take good care of each other. But she doesn't feel obligated to live her life in exactly the way they might have wanted if they were alive. She is focused on living for the living. In her own words: "The biggest change for me is realizing that more than anything, I want to *live* my life, not just pass through in a daze. And that though I'd like to have my parents, I don't *need* them."

Grief is not a single feeling, a pure tone of emotion. It is many feelings mixed together, a different mixture for each loss. It's important to be able to sift through this mixture and get a closer look at what's there: sadness, love, anger, gratitude, fear, comfort, and longing. Only by understanding the fullness of these emotions, and of the relationships that spawned them, is it possible to build a new life on a solid foundation of understanding and self-awareness after a death. Lisa, Barbara, and Rachael all had to spend some time looking back before they could look ahead, untangling the threads of what had been before weaving a new life for themselves.

For Rachael and Barbara, understanding meant recognizing a good dose of anger toward those they had loved and lost—anger rooted in dependence and painful to express because it existed within the context of generally loving relationships. For other people, the anger is right at the surface, and softer feelings are what seem to have been lost, if they were ever there at all. Faced with so much anger, people can't understand why it should be hard for them to let go of the person who provoked it. Yet they can't. This is the issue we'll turn to next.

CHAPTER 3

When Relationships Are Complicated, So Is Grief

Death ends a life, but it does not end a relationship, which struggles on in the survivor's mind toward some final resolution, some clear meaning, which it perhaps never finds.
—Robert Anderson, *I Never Sang for My Father*

I don't want to examine my relationship with my father. I want to have had a living father who loved me and a dead father who was my hero.
—Geneen Roth, *The Craggy Hole in My Heart and the Cat Who Fixed It*

*I*f only people were as easy to read, as simple to classify, as they are in our dreams, or in fairy tales. If they were, we would know who to hate and who to love, who to part from with relief and who to mourn. But the reality of human beings, and human relationships, is very different. Some people in our lives inspire powerful and powerfully divergent feelings. Usually they are the people to whom we are closest, people whose actions and words affect us deeply, for better or worse. Try as we might, when someone we love and trust injures us, we cannot whittle down our response to one of indifference. Once our heart is open to love, it is also open to hurt. And once open, it does not simply close when death ends a relationship with the living person.

Geneen Roth's quote at the beginning of this chapter is similar to the sentiments I often hear from mourners who hold ambivalent feelings about a loved one who has died. In other words, they hold both positive and negative feelings at the same time. Often, they would rather not think about the complexity of their feelings, particularly now that thinking about the difficult parts of the relationship seems a waste of time. Rather than struggle to understand the past, they would rather put it behind them; why dwell on what you can't change? Yet, as we saw with those in dependent relationships, this is precisely how people get stuck. Because in fact, they do continue to dwell on it and try to make sense of it, to work out the problems they could not resolve when the person was alive. But they can find no answers that satisfy them, no explanation for the person's behavior or for their own powerful and unrelenting grief.

Few human relationships are without some degree of ambivalence, some combination of contradictory emotions: love and gratitude coexist with anger and resentment. Many people understand and accept this feature of relationships while a person is alive, but find it uncomfortable to confront their negative feelings once someone has died. After all, the person is dead. Why bother?

One reason is remembrance: when we close our eyes to one set of feelings about a person, we may lose our ability to see that person at all: cutting ourselves off from memory, we cannot always choose what parts of our recollections are excised. Because the history of a loved one who has died is also our history, we may lose a piece of ourselves as well. It's difficult to build a sense of self, to build a life, on a foundation of half-truths and suppressed feelings. Further, it has been my experience that whatever feelings a mourner is trying to suppress tend to leak out in their other relationships. Anger toward a parent or spouse who has died may be directed at friends, children, or at ourselves.

I find great meaning in these often-quoted words from the Gospel according to Thomas: "If you bring forth what is inside you, what is inside you will save you. If you do not bring forth what is inside you, what is inside you will destroy you." I am reminded of this bit of wisdom when I meet someone who has been trying to deny feelings he or she regards as inappropriate or wrong about a loved one who has died, such as anger or resentment. Feelings are signals, and if we ignore them, they continue to try to break through any way they can. Anger that is not acknowledged is directed at someone who doesn't deserve it or at ourselves, or we get depressed, or our bodies take the hit and we develop mysterious aches and ailments. It's possible to continue to function, and many people do: they get up, go to work, cook dinner. People get by, they go on with their lives. But the lives of those who move on without reflection—particularly when their feelings are complicated and ambivalent—are neither as full nor as fulfilling as they could be. People with unacknowledged anger tend to re-create the problems of their old relationships in their new relationships and to continually reexperience the very emotions they have been trying to avoid.

It is true that once a loved one has died, we cannot hope to change the person or to know what he or she really thought or felt. But we can hope to confront and understand the full range of our *own* thoughts, feelings, and beliefs about the relationship. It is essential that we do so, not only to come to grips with the death of someone we loved, but to gain a new understanding of who we were with that person, who we are now, and how we will build a new life.

How Ambivalence Interferes with Mourning

WE SAW IN the last chapter how people in dependent relationships tend to get stuck in the first stage of mourning, acknowledging that a loss has occurred. People whose grief is complicated by ambivalence tend to get stuck in the second stage of mourning: fully confronting the loss. In the first stage of mourning, the task is to recognize the painful, irrevocable reality of death. In the second stage, the mourner struggles to confront all that the loss means for him or her in a practical and emotional sense. "These are the things he was," we say to ourselves. "This is what we loved to do together. This is who I was when he was in my life."

For many people, the second stage of mourning is the most difficult: numbness and disbelief melt away, only to be replaced by painful awareness. This pain, the unavoidable consequence of experiencing fully the impact of a loved one's death, is the true beginning of healing. When the funeral is over and the other mourners have gone back to their lives, when we finally have time to ourselves, two things happen: we hurt, and we heal. The two go together. Little by little we begin to map the landscape of our loss, a landscape made up of memories and the feelings they evoke. Some memories are beautiful. Some are hard to bear. Some are hard to bear *because* of their beauty. Other feelings may be difficult to tolerate, or even to acknowledge.

Ambivalence is an inescapable feature of many intimate relationships, simply because they *are* intimate. Like a close-up photograph, a close-up relationship allows us to appreciate both the beauty and the imperfections of the object of our attention, and we respond to both. As human beings, we are capable of loving deeply while at the same time feeling deep, passionate resentment, or frustration, or guilt, or fear. We respond to how people treat us, and they do not always treat us well. Nor are our responses always fair or compassionate. Human beings have a wide range of emotional responses: we are kind, we are devoted; we lose our tempers, we are resentful. Those we mourn were human, and we are human. The result of all of this humanness is often powerful and divergent feelings, feelings that remain after someone dies. Many people who mourn understand this in theory but still find it hard to remember or speak of times when their loved one hurt them or to admit to feeling anger or other emotions that seem at odds with the way they would like to remember the person or believe the person should be remembered. People can be more or less aware of editing their feelings: the process can be conscious or unconscious. There are people who insist that their husband was perfect, only to acknowledge after a period of time the remembered conflicts or disappointments. I have also had people tell me straight out that the relationship was difficult, but they still don't feel it's right for them to talk about it. I have heard, "I don't feel I have a right to be angry, I don't want to be angry, but I *am* angry." And that's the problem: feelings persist, whether they are wanted or not. Ignoring them, glossing over the difficult parts of a relationship, only makes the relationship hard to understand. And most people find it hard to accept what they can't understand.

The more powerful and divergent the feelings, the more uncomfortable they make us and the harder it is for us to make sense of them and to assemble a coherent picture of the person we are mourning. There is a name for the feeling evoked by this divergence: *dissonance*. Dissonance is that uncomfortable state of mind that arises when we are faced with evidence that contradicts a deeply held belief. When faced with dissonance, our minds want to simplify. We want something solid, something we can hold on to, something that isn't continually shifting back and forth, requiring us to reevaluate and question. So people try to exclude one half of the truth, to ignore those thoughts and feelings that conflict with the world as they believe it to be or would like it to be. They may try to stick with a version of events that, while not quite accurate, is simpler to understand and accept. But this strategy is dangerous, because at some level people know that what they're seeing is only half of the picture. Their mind is inevitably drawn to the other half, and the whole cycle begins again. Unavoidably, attempts to suppress part of what we know will result in confusion and unrest, like being on a mental seesaw. The effort to simplify the relationship, to view it as all bad or all good, only perpetuates our struggle to understand it and to make sense of our feelings about it. So it is that a woman whose husband who has just died will tell me that her husband was a bastard, only to wonder why, if he was such a bastard, she's sad that he's dead. Alternately, if someone's husband was so great, why is she so angry? This was the question that arose for Barbara when she talked about her marriage to Bob. At first Barbara talked about how Bob used to take care of everything for her; only later did she let on that he didn't always take care of things very well.

Confronting our full range of feelings takes energy, and in the early months of mourning it can feel like we just don't have it in us. But over time, avoiding or suppressing feelings saps energy too, and can deepen our sense of hopelessness. The decision to explore our full range of feelings can be a painful choice. It can take time, courage, and support from others. It can be hard. But often facing the truth is precisely what allows someone who has been stuck in grief to move on toward healing.

MICHAEL: Dealing with Dissonance

THE DEATH OF a loved one destroys a world—the shared world of a living relationship. The stories, the compromises, the understand-ings that may have worked to hold a relationship together—think about Barbara and Bob—can lose their usefulness or even become damaging once that relationship is ended by death. As we review the life we had with someone, we come face-to-face with all the complexity and contradictions that human relationships embody.

Thoughts and feelings bubble to the surface, drift down again, and are combined in unfamiliar and sometimes frightening ways. The result is emotional instability, but also emotional possibility—the possibility that ultimately can lead to positive changes in how we live our lives and understand ourselves.

I can think of no better example of this than Michael, a client I saw only a few times. Michael was mourning the death of his father. In our first meeting, Michael described him as "everything a husband and a father should be." By Michael's account, his father had been a larger-than-life figure: extremely successful in business and a pillar of the community. I'll never know of course who or what his father may have been to others, but to Michael he was all-powerful and all-knowing. From what I could gather, this was how his father had encouraged others, particularly his children, to regard him. Michael and his siblings understood full well that their father was not to be questioned. Not that he was entirely unapproachable, but when he was approached it was for advice, not complaint. Michael had not had an unhappy childhood. His father was not an ogre, just a strong, demanding, traditional sort who was set in his ways. Michael did not doubt that his father had loved him and cared about him and the rest of his family.

The problem Michael faced was that when he compared himself with his father, which he often did, he always came out feeling like the lesser man. Michael never saw his father cry; Michael was an emotional person who cried when he was upset and cried long and often over his father's death. Michael's father had been successful in business, and Michael had grown up in a big house in an exclusive neighborhood; Michael had doubts about his career and was considering moving his family to a less expensive town. His father "never questioned a decision"; Michael questioned himself every step of the way. So if Michael's father was "everything a husband and father should be," what did that make Michael?

Not surprisingly, in his mind Michael was a bad husband and provider, a terrible father and miserable example for his own sons. Again, I have no way of knowing for sure, but from the way he described his wife and children and his interactions with them, I would be very surprised if they shared his assessment.

To an outside observer, it was clear that Michael had both positive and negative feelings about his father. How could he not? When pressed, Michael remembered times when his father had been emotionally unavailable and demanding. But he had been raised by his father with a very specific concept of what constituted a good husband and father, and to believe that his father was the very model that defined the concept. Under the stress of his father's death, it was this model that prevailed in Michael's mind. Think of it as his default model. So if his father was all that was good, how could Michael, so different from his father, be anything but bad? In the worldview he had absorbed as a child, there was no room for Michael's father to be good and someone like Michael to also be good. Or for them both to be at least OK. Or for his father to have been damaging to others and for Michael to be a good and loving man valued by those around him. Who knows where the truth lay, exactly? I understood Michael's desire to honor his father's memory: certainly he had worked hard to provide a good life for his family. But from all I'd heard, I could not help but think that his father was not so perfect, nor Michael so despicable, as he believed. Why was it so hard for him to take pride in his own strengths or to acknowledge his father's shortcomings?

To fully answer that question I would need to get into the details of Michael's relationship with his father, a man who regarded himself as the absolute head of the family and insisted that his wife and children do the same. But even without these details, it's clear that after his father's death, Michael tried to carry on this tradition of unquestioning loyalty and respect for his father, whatever the cost. Rather than try to hold opposing beliefs, Michael interpreted all the events in his life to fit the clear and simple worldview that had been passed down to him by his father. His father's death was yet another in a string of events to be viewed through that lens, although doing so made it hard for Michael to go on with his life. After all, the person on whom he had based his understanding of how to live, who had provided the definition of what it meant to be a man, was gone. From now on, Michael would have to do the defining for himself. This created a crisis for Michael, but also an opportunity.

Having heard in detail all about his father's accomplishments and strengths, I asked Michael to fill in the details of his relationship with his father, a subject he had only touched upon. I asked Michael to tell me more about his memories of times when his father might have been less than perfect. I also asked him to tell me more about his close relationships with his own children and pointed out the contrast between his ability to connect with them and his father's difficulty showing and receiving love. In effect, I encouraged him to consider evidence that challenged his father's single-minded view of things. Michael was open to this, open to considering the possibility that he might be offering his wife and children a closeness and a richness that was different from what his father had provided but perhaps even more valuable. He also was open to the idea that he was comparing himself to an imagined giant. This was enough to move Michael along in his mourning, to at least get past the point where he could not help crying about his father's death, then berating himself for crying and entering a downward spiral that found him stuck ever more deeply in his grief. I didn't see Michael long enough to learn more, but his openness and willingness to consider alternative views of the world boded well for his emotional development and recovery from grief.

Michael's story reminds us that exaggerating someone else's strengths can lead us to exaggerate our own weaknesses. Remembering his father as unfailingly in control made Michael feel ashamed of his uncertainty, his mistakes, even his grief. Similarly, a woman who remembers her mother as always patient, kind, and good is likely to feel ashamed of what she sees as her own imperfections and selfishness. Put another way, if our memories of another person are inaccurate or distorted, and we use these memories to help us understand ourselves, we are bound to have a distorted sense of who we are.[1] While all this makes perfect sense in theory, remembering realistically—a prerequisite to getting unstuck—can be hard for all sorts of reasons. In the stories that follow, we'll look at three of the more common: anger and guilt (they almost always are paired); fear of what the truth might reveal; and deeply conflicted beliefs.

THERESA: Anger and Guilt

WHILE IT'S POSSIBLE for a person to have unacknowledged or unwanted positive feelings about someone who has died (we'll see an example of this later in this chapter), usually it's the negative feelings that are hardest for us to accept. This is not surprising when you consider that from childhood, most people are taught to regard negative feelings as unacceptable ("Don't say that! You don't *really* hate your brother/father/friend/me!").

Most often these feelings are some variation of anger: resentment, frustration, disillusionment. They can be directed at the person who has died or at ourselves. When we direct them inward, we often wind up with some variation of guilt: remorse, regret, shame. Many people who are ambivalent in their feelings toward someone who has died bounce between these poles of negative emotion, alternately blaming themselves and then blaming the deceased for problems in their relationship. This shifting back and forth between anger and guilt will continue until the mind finds a way to hold both thoughts at once; until the mourner is able to confront and ultimately reconcile these feelings. Sometimes, however, this process does not play itself out, and people get stuck—in anger, in guilt, in the dance between the two.

Guilt may be the most intractable of human emotions. How much easier it can be to forgive someone else whose behavior has been less than kind or attentive than it is to forgive our own lapses of thoughtfulness. This can be especially true for those who become caregivers to people they love. Tending to someone who is ill or dying draws upon all the caregiver's emotional and physical resources. While it can be gratifying, it is the rare individual who never feels exhausted, impatient, or desperate for time away from the sickbed. Unfortunately, it often happens that after a person dies, what stays with the survivor is not the multitude of times when he or she gave all and then some. Instead, people tend to dwell on those occasions when their patience and stamina gave out, nerves came unraveled, attention wavered: the times they yelled, didn't bring the glass of water, or went out with friends and missed the phone call. There may have been moments of resentment, even fleeting thoughts of how much easier life would be after the person's death. Most people would regard these reactions as understandable given the demands of caring for someone who is sick or dying. The truth is, though, that most of these same people would probably fault *themselves* for behavior they would forgive in someone else. Perhaps it is only to be expected that when someone dies, we are bound to feel that we could have done better, should have done better. Sadly, though, some people continue to tell themselves this for months, or even years, afterward.

When Theresa, sixty, first came to see me, her brother Peter had died a year and a half earlier. Peter had had Down syndrome and had lived in a halfway house for fifteen years after the death of their mother. At our first meeting, Theresa described her lifelong struggle with anxiety and her efforts to get it under control. Since her brother's death, her symptoms, including debilitating headaches, shoulder pain, and insomnia, had worsened. Under the care of a psychiatrist, she had tried different medications and recently had started hypnotherapy and relaxation techniques that led to sustained "crying jags." Theresa constantly was beset by negative thoughts about herself and regrets about Peter.

> As time goes by I just seem to get worse. The last two weeks have been very bad. I keep remembering how mean I was to Peter, how I yelled at him and made him cry.

Theresa wanted desperately to be able to relax, to get a break from the constant stream of chatter in her brain: the self-criticism, the worrying, her fear that she was going crazy.

We started our work by focusing on bringing down Theresa's level of anxiety. Given the many efforts she had made over the years to do this, I was not at all sure of what success we would have, and I admitted as much. "If this was a simple problem, you would have solved it by now. The fact that you haven't only tells me that it is a very tough problem." To give Theresa some hope about the possibility of relief, we practiced a combination of breathing techniques and visualization, always emphasizing Theresa's ability to help herself feel calmer and more relaxed. I made some other suggestions: daily exercise, a healthier diet, little or no alcohol.

Theresa's sense of relief was neither immediate nor complete. However, she was somewhat open to the suggestion that she be more gentle with herself—that she begin to guide her thoughts and behaviors in a different, more compassionate direction. In making this suggestion, my hope was that Theresa would begin to create a new narrative about herself and her relationship with Peter.

We began with Theresa's belief that her treatment of Peter "proved that [she] was a bad person": the times she lost her temper or made him cry. "He asked for so little. Why couldn't I just give him whatever he wanted?"

It was true that Peter's needs were simple, but caring for him was not. He would come for weekend visits with a bag full of dirty laundry, in need of a bath. Inevitably, Theresa would become frustrated with Peter's appearance or habits at some point during his visit and would express this frustration, sometimes more vehemently than she had intended. At this point Peter would begin to cry, and Theresa would vow to herself not to hurt him again. A quiet woman who valued her privacy, Theresa was in the unfamiliar position of being responsible for someone who needed considerable attention and caretaking, and the strain was difficult for her to manage, despite her love for her brother.

Rather than point out to Theresa that providing care for someone like her brother is stressful, that in fact she was the only one of her sisters to take Peter home for the weekend, I encouraged her to remember in more detail the happy times they had spent together. I began by asking, "Did Peter like coming to your house?"

Oh yes, he loved it. At night before he went to sleep we'd sing. He loved Broadway show tunes, and we sang a lot of those. He loved to play board games. He loved to laugh, and he laughed a lot at my house. Sometimes I'm astounded by how many pictures I have of him, and he looks *happy*.

Theresa talked about Peter's last weeks, when she had visited him in the hospital, held his hand, talked to him, and comforted him. At the conclusion of this session Theresa said that while she wasn't quite ready to do it, she wanted more than anything to keep working toward being more at peace with herself, "to let go of guilt about Peter, to let go of things I have no control over."

Like many people who feel overwhelmed by guilt after someone has died, Theresa saw her failure to be more compassionate with her brother as confirmation of every negative belief she had ever held about herself, further evidence that she was weak, selfish, incapable of putting someone else's needs ahead of her own. Much of what was in fact troubling Theresa was her anger. Yes, she admitted, she had sometimes resented Peter for needing her so much. And yes, there was some relief in his being gone. But what kind of person felt this way, she asked? What kind of person couldn't find it in her heart to forgive someone who couldn't take care of himself? Theresa found herself on an emotional merry-go-round, starting at anger, following her anger around until it turned into guilt, and escaping her guilt only to find herself back at anger.

Theresa was particularly loath to recognize her own anger and frustration because, after all, how could she be angry at her Down syndrome brother, who in reality was not fully responsible for his own actions? Well, she was and she wasn't. Of course she was angry at him sometimes, because she is human and because he was not entirely without the ability to control his behavior. But Theresa wasn't just angry at Peter. As we talked, it became clear she was angry about a lot of things related to Peter. She was mad at her siblings for not taking more responsibility for him; at the halfway house for not taking better care of him; at the fact that she lost control over her life when Peter was around; at her parents for not providing for better care for him before and after their death; and at God for making him the way he was and giving her the responsibility of being his caregiver.

Some of these feelings were more acceptable to Theresa than others, and together we focused first on those. It was some time before we moved on to look at how Theresa's childhood and adult family relationships affected her view of herself. For now, it was enough for her to recognize that she had brought a great deal of happiness into Peter's life and to understand that at least some of the anger she felt—not necessarily the anger she had directed toward him—was justifiable. With this understanding, Theresa was able to stop obsessing about her treatment of Peter. She was able to move forward in her mourning, to break the cycle of guilt and anger and position herself to again tackle the deeper emotional challenges she faced, many of which were unrelated to her brother's difficult life and death.

Interestingly enough, the experience of fully mourning Peter's death ultimately strengthened Theresa. It gave her a new confidence that she could deal with her own anxiety, and she made great progress in the months and years ahead. It is this more than anything else, I think—our human capacity to grow, in response to the internal pressure generated by the altered circumstances of our lives—that makes the experience of loss bearable and even affirming.

JASON: Fear

OF THE MANY reasons people have difficulty coming to grips with ambivalent feelings after the death of a loved one, fear can be the toughest to take on. By their nature, the things we fear often lie hidden in the depths of our unconscious. We don't like to disturb them, don't like to offer them up for analysis and evaluation. It always seems safer to let them be. But like every other emotion, fear is a signal, one that is unlikely to go away unless we attend to it. If it is not recognized and confronted, fear can make it hard for a person to mourn fully; fear makes it hard to remember the past realistically, harder still to imagine moving into the future.

Why is it that we're afraid of certain thoughts or feelings about a loved one who has died? Generally, the answer is that we're afraid of what those thoughts might say about that person, about the relationship we had with him or her, or about ourselves. It may be something we know is true but don't want to accept. Or it may be something we simply *fear* is true, a suspicion we're afraid we might confirm if we delve too deeply into our own thoughts.

Fear was not the issue that first came to mind when I met Jason, a twenty-year-old who came to see me several months after his girlfriend was killed in a car crash. When he walked into my office, I didn't quite know what to make of this very large, self-conscious guy in baggy pants and a backward baseball cap. The word *slacker* came to mind, quite unfairly as it turned out. As it was, I would learn a lot from Jason about how people can confound our initial judgments.

Delia had been Jason's first and only girlfriend. She was the first girl who had paid attention to him, made him feel attractive and wanted. He described her as his soul mate, his best friend, the one woman who loved him despite his being overweight, the only one who saw past his exterior and loved who he was inside. He was certain he would never find another woman as perfect, another relationship as easy and natural, as free of conflict.

To lose anyone we love is painful. To lose the first person you loved, and who loved you in return, is a terrible emotional injury for anyone to sustain. For Jason, who saw himself as generally unlovable and unattractive, Delia's death was devastating. He did not want to live without her and could not conceive of ever being with someone else or loving someone else.

If you ever were twenty and in love, you may be able to imagine how Jason felt. You may also be thinking, "Well, of course he believed she was perfect. He was young, she was his first girlfriend, and she died before anything could go wrong." But it wasn't quite that simple. What struck me about Jason, along with the depth of his sorrow, was how little he thought of himself, how the experience with Delia, rather than providing some evidence that he could love and be loved, had only confirmed his poor opinion of himself. Wouldn't love, the kind of unconditional love Jason described, make someone feel *more* loveable? If a person lost a love like that, wouldn't he or she somewhere, along with the sorrow, hold on to the belief that he or she could be loved again?

Jason had told me enough about his history to give me an inkling of why he saw himself in such a negative light. His father had abandoned him and his mother when Jason was a child. In school, he had been teased relentlessly about his weight. Still, I couldn't help but wonder if there wasn't something about the relationship with Delia that Jason was holding back, something that had disappointed him or made him angry.

In fact, Jason was angry a lot of the time. Mostly the anger was directed at his mother. They had always been very close, but since Delia's death he had argued with her continually. "I know I'm taking my anger out on her. I don't care," he admitted. He was also angry at his friends, most of whom he now regarded as phonies who didn't understand or care about him. He spent a lot of time talking about the falseness of people around him and his need to be constantly on alert for people whose actions did not match their words.

Many months after Delia's death, Jason was still feeling very depressed, still arguing with his mother, still coming home and talking to Delia's pictures, still replaying the details of their precious time together. In our sessions, he talked about the things he missed about Delia and described himself as worn out by the pain of his grief.

After several months of pretty much the same discussion, Jason started talking about his growing awareness of himself as a sensitive person, "even more sensitive than Delia." He described dreams in which he was trying unsuccessfully to connect with Delia, but she wasn't home, she wasn't answering the phone, or she didn't hear the phone ringing. I asked Jason if the frustration he felt in those dreams felt familiar to him. Had Delia ever not returned his phone calls or not been there when he needed her? He acknowledged that this had happened more than once. Jason had been frustrated by Delia's desire for time away from him and had often felt that he needed Delia more than she needed him. Returning to the dream, he spoke of "trying to get something from her, but I don't know what."

As Jason continued to talk about his feelings—*all* of his feelings—what emerged was a more complicated picture of his relationship with Delia, and of Jason himself. A few weeks before her death, Delia had told him she needed some space, and he reluctantly had agreed. He had struggled to be more accepting of her distancing so that she wouldn't leave him entirely, but she had started to see other men, and this had made him very angry and distraught and led to arguments between them. Now that she was gone, he blamed himself for driving her away out of his own neediness and anger.

As the full story emerged, I encouraged Jason to write about his thoughts and memories, and he took some comfort in the fact that this would help him remember what he and Delia had had together. He also began talking and writing about his episodic contact with his father and about his mother, toward whom he felt deep love, gratitude, and respect. The better I got to know him, the more I came to see Jason as someone capable of great emotional openness, honesty, and depth, someone earnest in his desire for a committed, loving relationship. Over time, he began to see himself in the same way. His relationship with his mother improved. He began making plans to go to college. He started seeing his friends again, exercising, and otherwise living his life.

Over time, Jason no longer needed the idealized version he had created of Delia and their relationship. For a while, the story had served an important purpose for him, because it was evidence that he had been loved. He felt it might have been an aberration, a one-time shot never to be repeated, but he had been loved, and the woman who had loved him had been tragically taken from him.

The story he had so feared, the real story as it turned out, was somewhat less romantic, though no less tragic for either of them. Delia might well have loved Jason, but had started seeing other people before her death. She had not loved him as much as he had loved her or needed him as much. That story, while true, was simply too much for Jason to take in the wake of her death because of what he feared it might say about him: that he was not lovable, never had been loved for who he was, and never would be. So he suppressed part of the story, wrote a new story, and spent whatever psychological energy it took to support it. It was one thing to tell this story to a therapist, or to his mother. But over time, the effort of suppressing memories, of failing to access the full range of his thoughts and feelings, was becoming exhausting. His anger at Delia as she pulled away from him, the heartbreak of seeing her with other men, and ultimately the fear that he was unlovable had to come to the surface to heal—and ultimately did. But in the immediate wake of Delia's death, he was not ready to accept these thoughts, and some part of his mind knew it.

With some help, Jason began to see that just because the "lost love" story he had created for himself was not going to hold up, this did not mean that the story line he most feared—the "unlovable man" story—was the whole truth either. He came to understand that much of the story of his life remained to be written and that he, the central character, was a worthwhile, talented young man who had discovered that while he wanted to build a life with someone, he could also stand on his own until the right person came along. Even when she did, Jason had a different idea about what he wanted from a relationship: "I'll always love and miss Delia," Jason told me a year after her death. "But I don't think that I ever want to be as dependent on one person as I was on Delia."

However much Jason learned about himself and his potential for happiness, he never let me forget that he would give it all up—would give anything—if it would bring Delia back to him. But little by little he came to grips with the fact that this was not going to happen, that nothing he could do would make it happen. Accepting this, he was gradually able to put more energy into building a life with meaning, a life in which he could put his talents to use, a life in which his love would not go to waste.

SUZANNE: Deeply Conflicted Grief

IN MY WORK and in my life, I have come to appreciate the variety, depth, and complexity of human relationships. In a book like this I can try to categorize people's problems and to present you with cases that more or less fit into one or another category, but the fact is that things are rarely that neat. Ambivalence is a broad category, capturing a range of problems that arise from conflicted remembrances and emotions about a loved one who has died. Dissonance, guilt, anger, and fear often reside within the same person's mind.

Suzanne, whom you met in Chapter 1, had elements of all these issues. What makes Suzanne's story such a good one to illustrate ambivalence is that all these feelings stemmed from a relationship in which the dissonant aspects—the love and the fury—were each felt so intensely, and were so evenly balanced, that Suzanne truly did not know what to think or how to proceed. Dissonant feelings are tough to come to grips with under any circumstances. The mind rebels at the idea of holding two opposing emotions at once. Michael, Theresa, and Jason had underlying resentments toward the people they had lost and for different reasons had a tough time bringing the more negative feelings to the surface. Suzanne did not have this problem. She was able to identify the good and the bad in her mother and in their relationship. What she couldn't understand was why she was still so absorbed by her grief. Finding herself caught between two extremes of emotion, Suzanne could not understand the depth of her grief and why it didn't seem to be getting any less intense with time.

Suzanne, sixty-two when I met her, was married, with children and grandchildren. Her mother had died five months before she came to see me. Two years before she died, Suzanne's mother had broken her hip and spent time in a convalescent center. While there, she contracted pneumonia and developed a respiratory infection. She was put on oxygen and remained on it when she was sent home, where she was cared for by Suzanne's brother. Once at home,

Suzanne's mother resumed her lifelong habit of smoking, despite her doctor's warnings and Suzanne's pleas that she stop. One night, she fell asleep in her bed with a lit cigarette. The oxygen ignited, and in the resulting conflagration, Suzanne's mother received third-degree burns from which she died a week later.

Suzanne's mother's death marked the end of a life marred by depression, alcoholism, and domestic violence. Suzanne's grief was complicated by her sorrow about all that her mother had suffered, her sense that all that her mother had known was trouble and pain. Since her mother's death, Suzanne had been experiencing intense sorrow and grief. She found herself crying regularly and uncontrollably about her mother's death and thinking about it day and night. "I can't stop thinking about it," she said, "It seems like it's all I think about."

What Suzanne found hardest to understand was why she felt as bad as she did. She hadn't expected to. Suzanne described her relationship with her mother as almost too close, "joined at the hip," but she had no illusions about who her mother had been or how she had treated Suzanne. In between her tears, Suzanne berated herself for feeling so sad about a woman who had seldom had a kind word for her, but who had no trouble expressing anger and disapproval:

> I keep asking myself—why am I still grieving my mother? When she was alive . . . my mother made me feel like the worst piece of crap on earth. Why can't I let her go? Why?

Suzanne filled in the details as she remembered them. Her mother had been an alcoholic. She had had no time for Suzanne. Suzanne could not remember a specific occasion on which her mother had kissed her. Her mother had not attended Suzanne's high school graduation or other important events as she was growing up. She had suffered from severe depression and had more than once been admitted to a psychiatric hospital. Suzanne left home at sixteen, seeking consolation in a relationship that resulted in her becoming pregnant.

Given what she was telling me, it was clear that her mother's death had opened a lot of old wounds for Suzanne. But why was she feeling *so* bad after months and months and showing no signs of recovering from her intense grief?

Despite her anger toward her mother, Suzanne had never stopped loving her and had never broken off contact with her. Moreover, it was clear that Suzanne had always felt a deep sense of responsibility for her mother. I asked Suzanne if there had been a time in her life when she had felt she needed to protect her mother. She immediately recalled a time as a child when her mother and father were arguing and her father threw her mother to the floor and started hitting her. Recalling this, Suzanne said simply, "It was scary. I was scared." Suzanne also recalled a time, when she was in high school, that her mother had locked herself in the bathroom and threatened to cut her wrists.

It is not unusual for children of parents with problems—drugs, alcohol, depression—to feel that they must protect their parent at all costs. The feeling is reasonable enough: young children, after all, are not capable of caring for themselves. Life with a depressed, angry parent is scary, but known. Life without that parent is scary and unknown. Suzanne was conditioned through a lifetime of close calls to believe that she needed to take personal responsibility for keeping her mother alive.

Suzanne felt guilty about being unable to stop her mother from smoking after she returned home from the hospital. When smoking led directly to her death, Suzanne took a big part of the blame onto herself. We talked about that and about her inability to stop thinking back on the day her mother died and her remorse that she had not been there when the end came. Suzanne had visited her mother in the hospital every day, including the day she died. On that day, she had returned to work after the visit with her mother and received a call from the hospital just a few hours later telling her of her mother's death. She could not forgive herself for not know-ing how close to death her mother had been. If only she had been there, Suzanne believed, maybe things would have been different. Maybe she could have saved her. Suzanne admitted that the doctor had given her no indication when she left the hospital that day that her mother might be dead in a few hours. I reminded her that it frequently happens that death comes at just the moment an attentive loved one leaves the hospital room to get a breath of fresh air or a meal. Suzanne knew all this, but it didn't seem to matter to her.

Suzanne believed she was responsible for protecting her mother, and from childhood on she had continued to carry this responsibility despite all that her mother did to put her life and health in jeopardy. For Suzanne, her mother's breakdowns, her close calls, were Suzanne's failures. In this sense, her mother's death was the ultimate failure, proof that she had not performed her lifelong job of keeping her mother alive.

Usually, these are not beliefs that a person carries around at a conscious level. As Suzanne told me more than once, "When I was growing up, and even later, I wasn't thinking about what was happening at the time. I was just living it." And that's just the point. Children don't always think about what's happening to them, but they do remember it. Moreover, as long as memories remain unconscious, they remain the memories of a child who experienced a painful event, like Suzanne's mother's suicide attempts and the violence between her mother and father. Hidden from conscious awareness, these memories are beyond the reach of adult reason, adult experience, and adult perspective.

Over time, Suzanne was able to get hold of these memories and look at them from the standpoint of her current, adult self. As she did, her guilt about not protecting her mother was tempered by the realization that a child should not be put in the position of protecting her parent, that adults are responsible for their own behavior, that her mother put herself at risk again and again despite all of Suzanne's efforts. Eventually, Suzanne came to see that even the accident that led to her mother's death had been self-inflicted and not something Suzanne could have prevented, any more than she could have prevented the other injuries and misfortunes of her mother's life.

> What happened at the end of her life almost feels like another suicide attempt. It's almost like she committed suicide with the cigarette. And that makes me think, why did she have to be that way. These things shouldn't have happened to me. They shouldn't have happened to my brother.

While this was an important breakthrough for Suzanne, she continued to ruminate about her mother's life and death. She asked, "Why can't I just let it go?" Frustrated but still determined, Suzanne returned again and again to the questions she had had for much of her life, questions about what drove her mother to act as she did, about why she was so unhappy, so intent on doing damage to herself. Without this understanding, Suzanne felt she could not recover from her grief. She was tortured by the idea that she would never be able to get over losing her mother because she had never really *had* her, had never really known her.

> I kept trying to change her, to get her to stop being so negative. Why couldn't she be different? I still don't understand why she had to be that way.

Suzanne had asked this last question—Why did she have to be that way?—throughout her mother's life. Now that her mother was dead, Suzanne was afraid it would plague her forever. As long as her mother lived, Suzanne had held out hope that she would change, would express love and appreciation, and would grow into someone Suzanne could love without reservation. Suzanne regretted that her mother did not "live long enough" to allow Suzanne to get close to her. Suzanne, remember, was in her sixties, and her mother eighty. Such hopes die hard.

Since the source of Suzanne's despair, as she described it, was her feeling that she had never known her mother, I thought it might be helpful if we could collect whatever information she *did* have: to help her focus on what she *did* know about her. Even though Suzanne had spent her adult life longing to know her mother, this was a frightening prospect. In remembering, she would get to know her as well as she ever would, and she might not like the picture that emerged. Once she made the commitment to remembering, the memories—and answers—began to flow.

As Suzanne talked about her mother over weeks and months, there were many remembered disappointments, many hurts and humiliations. There also were some surprises. Along with the painful memories, locked up beside them, were other memories, happier memories, and these began to come back to Suzanne as well.

In particular, Suzanne remembered a period of her childhood when her mother had been relatively healthy and happy. She remembered helping her hang up the laundry, the way the warm sheets smelled, her mother's laughter. She remembered her family spending Sunday afternoons at the lake with other families, the children playing together until long past sundown. She remembered how her mother had loved to sing to her and how beautiful her voice was. These memories, too, were hard for Suzanne to discuss, because along with them came the realization of all she and her mother could have had, a true taste of what she would yearn for for the rest of her life.

These were bittersweet recollections, but they helped explain why Suzanne had held so fiercely to the idea that her mother one day might change, as well as why those hopes had been so futile. In the end, the memories gave more comfort than distress, and they helped explain Suzanne's grief and pain in a way that made sense to her. Suzanne was coming to terms with all she felt and knew about her mother—not just the downtrodden and distant woman she had struggled to know, but the woman who had given her a glimpse of what might have been if things had been different.

Suzanne also talked more about her own past, her own mistakes and regrets. In particular, she talked about leaving home as a teenager and about the termination of her pregnancy. She ended the relationship with her boyfriend shortly after, a decision she recalled with remorse: "I knew it hurt him. But I didn't do it to hurt him. You don't intentionally set out to hurt people. Some people make mistakes. You are what you are. I didn't set out to be a bad person." Pausing a moment, Suzanne added, "I guess that goes for my mother, too."

Shortly after this meeting, Suzanne traveled to her childhood home and visited her mother's grave. She reported back that she had told her mother she was doing well, although sometimes the feelings were still intense. She said,

> I'm grieving my mother—what she had, what she didn't have, the good, the bad, the ugly. Sometimes it's too much, and if I think about the bad stuff I just want to block it out. But I don't want to forget it. Whatever I lived through I had to be strong to get through it. It made me a strong person.

This was not the end of Suzanne's work. She continued to sort through her memories and, like Jason, began writing some of them down. Writing helps move memories from the inside to the outside. Reading them makes it possible to remember difficult times without reliving them. It also relieves us of the need to continually replay our memories: we have them, they are there, they're not going to disappear. This can be just as important in the case of bad memories as it is for the good. As Suzanne observed, everything we go through plays a part in making us who we are. If we remember the past selectively, we cannot hope to have more than a fragmented understanding of ourselves.

There was a lot of disappointment, anger, and conflict in Suzanne's relationship with her mother. There was also love, longing, and regret. Why did Suzanne grieve so when her mother died?

Why did she dwell so on her mother's life and death? Why was she so confused about her own grief? As we've seen, the answers to these questions are as complex as the relationship. On the broadest level, Suzanne was beset by ambivalent feelings, feelings that seemed contradictory and eluded her ready understanding. Suzanne felt guilty about her mother's death and resentful that her mother had put her in a position to feel guilty. She felt sorrow for her mother, and she felt angry at her mother for the effect her difficulties—at least some of them self-imposed—had had on her and her brother. All her life Suzanne had held fast to the belief that with only a little more time her mother might have been different, might have known her; and her mother had died with these hopes still unfulfilled. At times she hated her mother for her coldness and her distance, but she also loved her mother and deep down guarded memories of a time when it seemed things just might turn out differently for them.

Suzanne was confused about her feelings after her mother's death because over the span of six decades together, she had experienced deeply and fully the entire range of human emotions in their relationship. What was she to feel now? Suzanne's mind simply could not hold all those emotions at once. It made no sense to her: "I try to be rational about this," she complained initially, "but I can't." She tried to simplify. She tried to ignore. In the end, she decided to remember, not just part but *all* that her mother had meant to her over the course of their life together. Layer by layer, her feelings began to make sense. Gradually, as she came to terms with the totality of her mother's life, she was able to come to terms with her death. Suzanne still thought about her mother sometimes, but most of the time she thought about other things: her husband, her children and grandchildren, her golf game. Suzanne was living again.

Talk and Remembrance

I'M OFTEN ASKED if just talking about a person who has died is enough. The answer is, *sometimes*. For each of the people described in this chapter, and indeed, for many people who have the kind of prolonged and intense grief described in this book, something besides talking can be helpful, and may be needed. Some of these approaches, like EMDR and imagery, will be discussed in the next chapter. Some are much simpler. For example, I encourage people to pay attention to what feelings come up in their bodies when they are describing an experience, because tuning in to these cues is a way of involving all of their thoughts, feelings, and sensations in the process of remembering.

People who are trying to manage painful and conflicting feelings often suffer from an extreme version of a problem that afflicts most of us at one time or another: rumination. In effect, their mental off-switch is temporarily broken. Their minds are constantly agitating, reviewing, evaluating, regretting. What I often suggest to people is that they try using some kind of strategy for quieting their minds. This can be as simple as taking a walk, listening to music, or sitting in a quiet place. Prayer can be a haven. Meditation and yoga are increasingly popular approaches to achieving a quieter, more centered state of being, and in fact they can help balance the emotionally exhausting work of recollecting and provide a much-needed rest for the spirit.

Mourning is about remembering. Acknowledging the imperfections of a relationship doesn't diminish its importance, nor does it mean that you would have been better off without that relationship. Remembering fully doesn't deprive you of the good parts of a relationship. In fact, the opposite is more often true: recollecting the relationship, the person, and your feelings in their entirety enables you to understand the meaning of what you have lost, to internalize a sense of who the person was, why the relationship was important to you, and what you will take from that relationship into your life from this point forward.

That's what happened for each of the people you've read about here. None of these relationships were simple. The more complicated they were, the harder it was for people to come to terms with their memories and the feelings they evoked. But they kept at it, and in doing so they were able to reclaim the energy they had been using to keep these unwanted feelings from full consciousness.

The next chapter is also about reclaiming what has been lost, but in a somewhat different sense. For people who are mourning the death of someone who neglected or abused them, what must be reclaimed may lie deep within them; its resurrection will require all their resources and courage.

CHAPTER 4

The Lasting Effects of Toxic
Relationships and Abuse

*The tectonic layers of our lives rest so tightly one on top of the
other that we always come up against earlier events in later
ones, not as matter that has been fully formed and pushed
aside, but absolutely present and alive. I understand this.
Nevertheless, I sometimes find it hard to bear.*
—Bernard Schlink, *The Reader*

The past is never dead. It's not even past.
—William Faulkner, *Requiem for a Nun*

In this chapter we'll talk about how the experience of abuse, particularly childhood abuse, can affect mourning. Even more than the people we met in the last chapter, who had ambivalent relationships with a loved one who died, people who suffer early abuse have a difficult time facing the full range of their feelings. But the difference is more than simply one of degree. When abuse has occurred, the toxicity of the emotions involved, added to the psychological damage caused by the abuse itself, can make it nearly impossible to engage in the mourning process without first addressing the underlying experience and lasting effects of abuse.

Experiencing abuse as a child, whether physical or psychological, is a form of trauma. Trauma is the body's response to circumstances or events we perceive as life threatening and out of our control. A car accident, a violent crime, a natural disaster: all these things can induce physical and emotional trauma in those who are involved in them or witness them. Trauma brings on a potent mixture of feelings: terror and helplessness combined. When experiencing trauma, the mind is flooded with all the chemicals that trigger the impulse to fight or flee, but there may be no way out.

Of all the different kinds of trauma, abuse may well be the most devastating because it is so intensely personal. Being hurt by someone you love, or watching people you love hurt each other, is as personal as it gets.[1]

Being in a car accident or being the victim of nature's fury can be painful, terrifying experiences that produce lasting effects. But by and large these are not events directed specifically at the person who suffers them. They just happen. What's known as *relational trauma*,[2] on the other hand, is inflicted on a specific person by someone close to him or her. It raises a whole different set of questions: not just "Why me?" in a general sense, but "Why is my father (or mother, or spouse) treating me this way? Why does he want to hurt me? What am I doing to make him so angry? What's wrong with me?" Relational trauma affects a person's self-image and assumptions about the world and what it has in store, and these effects can last a lifetime.

As we learned in Chapter 2, a healthy parental attachment provides a child with comfort and reassurance, a feeling of being safe in the world. Under the watchful eyes of a loving parent, a child can learn and practice smiling, crying, making contact—all the behaviors that make us human. When abuse is present, there can be no refuge, and a child is exposed to constant threat from the very people charged with his or her care and protection.

Jon Allen, a psychologist at the Menninger Institute, describes how early abuse creates a "dual liability, by creating extreme distress and undermining the development of capacities to regulate that distress." In other words, an abused child may never develop the coping skills he or she is most likely to need as an adult when facing life's inevitable stressors, like losing a loved one. Capabilities that come naturally to many people because they learned them by interacting with and observing their parents—the ability to self-sooth, to understand and tolerate strong emotions, to seek out social support—may not be part of the emotional repertoire of someone who was abused. Of course, many survivors of early abuse *do* learn these skills and develop the capacity to deal with the stresses of life and the emotions they produce. People can heal from painful, even horrific childhood experiences, but they may need help to do so.

Often, though not always, child victims of abuse simply will shut down their developing emotions. This may help them get through the moment, but the consequences are far-ranging and hard to undo. Once shut down, it isn't so easy to turn emotions back on again, or to know when it is appropriate to do so.

Children who are abused are focused on survival. They may go to great lengths to develop a kind of early warning system in hopes of avoiding harm, tuning in to a parent's subtle changes in facial expression or tone of voice. So, while their own emotional responses are shutting down, abused children may become hyper-attuned to the emotions of others. In fact they may become so focused on other people's feelings that their own feelings barely matter or register to them at all.

There is no one way that a "typical" survivor of abuse grows into adulthood, but there are some characteristics many survivors share. Abused children may well grow up not really knowing what they feel or what is important to them. Many suffer from depression. Having had no experience of a healthy, loving relationship—the kind of relationship that could be the ultimate antidote to their emotional deprivation—they may not know what to look for in a partner or recognize the potential for love when it presents itself. In fact, many people who were abused as children form adult relationships in which the deprivation and hurt of their childhood are re-created. They find partners who are quick to criticize, slow to forgive. Or they come to regard intimacy itself as unsafe and avoid forming close relationships at all. Sometimes, having learned early on the necessity of being constantly attuned to a parent's mood, they may grow up to be empathetic to a fault, considering everyone's wants and needs but their own. Sometimes they become abusers themselves.

When people who have been abused lose a loved one, particularly when that person was their abuser, they face two potential problems in mourning. The first is coming to grips with the full range of their emotions about that person. This task is complicated both by the extreme nature of the feelings involved and by the persistent impact on the survivor of early trauma. Many survivors, for example, begin to feel acutely anxious if they say anything against their abuser. Along with this, some survivors will need to learn the basic emotional skills they will need to build a new life for themselves, skills they never had the opportunity to learn as children.

All of this may sound daunting, and it can be, but it is far from impossible. The treatment of trauma, including the trauma of early abuse, is an area of psychology that has seen tremendous progress over the past three decades, giving us a whole new set of therapies for moderating some of trauma's most destructive effects. People who are mourning the loss of a relationship in which there was abuse may need extra help in dealing with their grief, but that help is available.

SUSAN: I Know What You're Saying Is True, But . . .

A LOT OF what a therapist might ordinarily do to help someone in mourning may not be of much use when trying to help a person who has suffered abuse. This is something I learned the hard way, early in my career as a therapist, when I found myself frustrated by my inability to help one particular person as much as I would have liked.

Susan walked into my office one day to talk to me about the difficulty she was having in coping with the death of her mother six months earlier. Susan was charming: articulate and with a quality I can only describe as genuine sweetness. I felt an immediate connection to this appealing young woman and hoped I would be able to help her.

Susan had been planning her wedding at the time of her mother's death, and she wanted to proceed with these plans, but things were not going at all smoothly. Understandably, Susan longed to have her mother beside her to help with preparations for this important day in her life. But what was more upsetting to Susan was that she was unable to shake the feeling that the marriage was doomed, that she would not be capable of keeping up her end of it. Susan explained that she had never had a healthy loving relationship with a man before meeting her future husband. She had avoided intimate relationships for much of her life and feared that her tendency to distance herself from those around her would ultimately drive her husband away.

Trying to understand the source of Susan's fears, I asked her to tell me about her family. What she described was horrible. Her father's verbal and physical abuse had been so severe that the children were removed from their home. Susan's mother had been unable to protect her children, and although Susan and her siblings eventually returned, each one left on their own as soon as they were of age.

Over the next month, Susan and I talked at length about what she had endured as a child and how it had distorted her feelings about herself, her value as a person, her ability to love and be loved. While she understood that what had happened to her as a child was not her fault, she could not stop feeling that the punishment she had been subjected to was somehow deserved. Surely, she thought, to have been treated this way she must have been a troublesome, messy, ungrateful child. With so much badness in her, how could she hope to be loved? How could she hope to have a happy marriage, to be a decent parent?

As an adult, Susan had become close to her mother. Her mother was the one person who could soothe her and reassure her that she was good and deserving of love. With her mother gone, Susan was incapable of sustaining these positive feelings about herself. Without her mother, Susan could not seem to shake the negative self-image that was her default mode: if anything went wrong, it must be because of some failure on her part. If anyone else criticized Susan, she was unable to realistically assess the truth or fairness of the criticism. She simply absorbed it and felt bad about herself.

I soon discovered that although talking about her past enabled Susan, in her words, to "understand in my head" why she was so hard on herself, she could not stop *feeling* like there was something wrong with her, something shameful. I was frustrated by my inability to help Susan feel compassion for herself for all she had been through and to believe deep down that the love she deserved was finally coming her way. We did what we could. Some time later, Susan told me that she and her fiancé would be relocating to another city. We talked about what she had accomplished, about her remaining concerns, and about how she could continue to cultivate good feelings about herself and her future.

I don't know what happened to Susan. I like to think that her essential good nature, the real strength and beauty in her, combined with the love of her new husband, went a long way toward repairing the damage of her childhood. But I was never satisfied with what I had done or failed to do. Years later, I still think about how I would do things differently if Susan were to walk into my office today.

Understanding Trauma

WHAT I LEARNED from Susan was that sometimes talk just isn't enough. It is one thing to understand something intellectually, and another to *feel* it, to believe it, to act differently and interact with others differently because something inside has shifted. That's what I wanted to help people to do, and eventually I learned that it is possible.

The key to helping people in Susan's position is to understand that the abuse they suffered was a trauma, a particularly devastating form of trauma, and that their mourning cannot fully unfold until the trauma and its long-term effects are addressed. Dealing with trauma, however, presents unique challenges.

Most people who walk through my office door are able to benefit from traditional "talk therapy." Having someone listen to their story empathically, being able to talk about their lost loved one without fear of being judged or being told to get over it, goes a long way toward helping many mourners.

In dealing with trauma, however, the most basic tool of talk therapy—language itself—can become a trap.[3] When people are encouraged to talk about a traumatic experience like abuse, whether by a well-intentioned therapist or a friend or family member, the discussion alone may inadvertently trigger symptoms of trauma, like flashbacks or severe anxiety. Even in the hands of a therapist with the skills to avoid these reactions, talk alone is unlikely to leave people actually *feeling* much different about themselves or the experience they have been through.

People who work with and write about trauma often talk about memories being "stored in the body" as well as the brain. As Babette Rothschild explains, this doesn't mean that memories are literally recorded "in bone and marrow." Rather, they are stored in parts of the brain that connect most directly to the body. As a result, later events that in some way are evocative of the original trauma are apt to cause the same physiological and emotional reactions, whether warranted or not.

Maggie Scarf, in her book *Secrets, Lies, Betrayals*, provides one of the more understandable explanations of how the brain reacts to trauma.[4] In a life-threatening situation, the limbic system takes over. Two little nutlike areas known as the amygdala send a signal to another area known as the hypothalamus, which initiates a series of reactions that put the body into a state of immediate readiness. Millions of years of evolution are put to work in a fraction of a second: the autonomic nervous system releases stress hormones that increase heart rate and blood pressure and the flow of oxygen to the muscles increases, all in preparation to fight, flee, or freeze.

There are situations in which these reactions are perfectly appropriate—times when this rapid-response alarm system is crucial to our survival. But false alarms are common. Once the limbic system has been triggered, events unrelated to the original trauma can trigger it again. Part of this has to do with how traumatic memories are stored. Traumatic memories are recorded as fragments, bits and pieces of experience—thoughts, feelings, body sensations—without a logical "narrative" that connects them to the past. They can, and do, invade the present, whether or not the person has any explicit memory of the original event. In other words, people who have suffered a trauma may feel terror, but have no idea why. Or they may "know" rationally that a situation differs from the traumatic experience, but still have the same response. For example, someone who witnessed the attacks on the World Trade Center may experience an ordinary event—a bird flying past his or her window—and have a momentary emotional and physical reaction more appropriate to that earlier, extraordinary event.

While people may be aware of some instances when these reactions are triggered, the likelihood is that there will be many situations that trigger a response without the person's being conscious of what is occurring. A woman feels a sharp pain in her stomach anytime she hears someone scream at a child; a man tenses anytime he hears a door slam.

Depending on the nature of the trauma and its duration, people who have experienced trauma may always be "on guard." On a fairly regular basis, their brain sends signals to tense this muscle or that, to shorten breath, to kick up the level of certain enzymes. Over time, this can take a toll on both mind and body. This is what it means for memories to be "stored in the body." They really are stored in the brain, but in such a way that they continue to directly affect a person's body and his or her emotional reactions. Understanding the body's responses on an intellectual level can help, and sometimes it helps a lot. But sometimes other techniques are needed to deal with the fundamental emotional and physical impact of trauma.

The study of traumatic stress intensified in the years following the Vietnam War, when large numbers of returning soldiers experienced a range of symptoms—flashbacks, night terrors, intrusive thoughts, panic responses—that left them miserable and interfered with their reintegration into civilian life. Psychologists working with these soldiers identified a set of persistent symptoms they termed post-traumatic stress disorder (PTSD), a diagnosis that came to be applied more generally to people who had experienced other types of trauma and exhibited similar symptoms.

Not everyone experiencing a traumatic event suffers from full-blown PTSD, or from any posttraumatic effects at all.[5] As you might expect, an event that might be mentally assimilated by one person may affect someone else entirely differently. Many soldiers experience combat, and for just about all the experience is terrifying and traumatic. Not all experience PTSD. The *post* in PTSD signifies that the mind/body reactions to the event have not receded with time; they persist long after the immediate danger associated with the trauma has passed. Even for those who are not diagnosed with PTSD, traumatic memories may remain in the body like shards of emotional glass, untempered by time. When triggered, they often are experienced as if the original event were happening in the moment.

Millions of people experience trauma, and some of the symptoms of PTSD, as a result of terrible but commonplace events like car crashes, accidents on the job, or becoming a victim of crime. Sometimes thousands of people can be affected at once, as with mass terror attacks. In fact, the very objective of terrorism is to inflict terror and helplessness—the definition of trauma—on an entire population.

In the next chapter, we'll talk about the impact of traumatic death on survivors and loved ones. Right now, let's get back to one particular type of trauma, abuse at the hands of a loved one, and its impact on mourning.

MARGARET

When Margaret first came into my office, she reminded me a little of Susan. She projected a warmth and directness I found immediately appealing. Margaret was an accomplished athlete and outdoorswoman. She combined her love of the wilderness with her work as a management coach, leading backwoods team-building retreats for businesspeople. She had an intense vitality that made you believe she was imbued with tremendous mental and physical confidence. And that was true, to an extent. But it also was true that Margaret often felt sad, had been through a series of unsatisfying relationships that had ended badly, and wondered why she spent so much of her time alone.

You may remember some of Margaret's story from Chapter 1. Margaret came to see me after her brother, Chris, had died in an automobile accident. More than anyone in her life, Chris had been the person Margaret could talk to about anything, the one who knew about all the pain of growing up with their physically and emotionally abusive father. Together, in their teens, both had turned to alcohol and drugs. Margaret had been the first to achieve sobriety. Chris's recent efforts to gain control of his life made his sudden death all the more difficult for Margaret to accept. Chris had been pulling his life together, and he and Margaret had made plans to renovate a two-family house they would share, giving Margaret a sense of hope for the future. With Chris's death, Margaret felt that she had lost that future, and she didn't know how she was going to see her way to finding a new one.

While she didn't realize it at the time, Chris's was not the only death she was mourning. Margaret had been in therapy on and off since the death of her father years ago. While she had talked about her father a lot during the course of her therapy, she had not dealt directly with his death, her feelings about his death, or the earlier pain he had inflicted on her and the rest of her family. In fact, she had come to feel that she spent much of her time in therapy "making excuses" for her father.

It is not unusual for people who start out by wanting to talk about a recent loss to find themselves talking about a great deal more. They come in to get help in coming to terms with one loss, but find that much of their sorrow goes back to earlier losses. In Margaret's case, there was her father's death, which was tied to still earlier losses: her own loss of innocence and loss of hope. Yet Margaret had survived. In fact, she was a "survivor" very much in the mold of those on reality TV shows: athletic, a wilderness trainer, afraid of nothing that nature might throw at her. But survival is not wholeness, or happiness, or fulfillment. Certainly, Margaret had had glimmers of all these things in her life, but she did not seem to be able to hold on to any of them for long, and she often found herself slipping into old feelings and behaviors.

Chris's death had triggered all of Margaret's most painful memories of her father and the feelings that inevitably went with them. She felt alone, and she was overwhelmed by a powerful sense that something terrible could, and would, happen at any moment.

In fact, something terrible *had* happened—her brother had died, calling up all of Margaret's fears, the learned responses of her childhood. These thoughts and feelings increasingly were interfering with her sleep, her work, her life. She was irritable, quick to anger. And she was very hard on herself. Guilt and shame were a recurring theme in much she wanted to talk about.

Like Margaret, Chris had loathed and feared their father, and in fact he had been the target of some of his father's worst abuse. Margaret was two years older than her brother, and many of her most vivid memories were not of her own abuse, which was crushing enough, but of her father mercilessly beating Chris. Recalling the details of several particularly horrific incidents triggered the same feelings of terror and helplessness she had suffered as a child and let loose a torrent of self-recrimination. If only she had been stronger, if only she had been able to stop her father from hurting her brother, how might his life have been different? How could she ever forgive herself for not saving him?

It was clear to me, as it would have been to any reasonable person hearing her story, that Margaret had nothing to feel guilty about. She was a small child. Her father was a powerful and emotionally dominating adult. There was nothing she could have done beyond what she did: hide, run, cry, and survive. Margaret understood this, but understanding it intellectually didn't keep her from feeling the same way she had felt then.

Another area of self-reproach to which Margaret continually returned was her inability to "make my father see who I was, who my brother was." Margaret believed that if only she had succeeded in doing so, "he wouldn't have hurt us." She held on to this belief despite the fact that her father had never shown any inclination toward compassion, and had never, in Margaret's memory, shown her the slightest bit of love or approval.

> I wanted to please this man so much because I thought that
> would work—that if I could make him see who I was he

would be pleased with me. All I ever wanted was to be good and be noticed for that. But it never turned out that way. I always felt inadequate. I always felt like a failure. I remember telling myself, I can't do anything right. But then I would tell myself I have to do better next time.

Throughout her father's life, Margaret had never given up trying to discover the code that would unlock his heart. Tough and composed on the outside, inside Margaret continued to feel frustrated and inadequate. Despite knowing at some level that her struggle to win over her father was futile, she couldn't give it up. Even when he was alive, a part of her knew that she never would or could break through to the heart of someone so cold, so mean to everyone around him. Now he had been dead for years, yet she still fantasized that if only he were alive, she might have a chance of doing the one right thing that would make him love her. Why, she wanted to know, despite years of talking about her father in therapy, did she still make excuses for him? How was it that she could still miss him?

As we saw in the last chapter, negative feelings and emotions can create as lasting a bond as love and respect. Unresolved conflicts are replayed over and over, unrequited hopes are nurtured and kept alive despite the fact that objectively death has stolen any opportunity, real or imagined, that may have existed to right a terrible wrong. This powerful bond of anger, bitterness, and regret is not easily broken. When Margaret's father died years ago, he took with him any possibility for Margaret to fulfill her deepest longing: that somehow she could make him see who she was, and simply love her. For years Margaret had been stuck in chronic mourning, unable to see that what she missed, what she longed for, was not her father as he really was, but the father she never had and never would have.

As Margaret described the events of her childhood, she seemed to fold in on herself, transforming before my eyes from a self-confident woman into a frightened child. "I think about what my father did, how he could just take over whatever was going on with his anger, just obliterate the rest of us with his rage. I just know that so much of that is still inside me. How could it not be?"

In one sense, Margaret's experience had pressed her to strengthen herself, literally to harden her body through wilderness experiences. But she had not hardened her heart. On the contrary, Margaret had become exquisitely attuned to the feelings of others. She was a good, compassionate, and caring friend. Yet she belittled even these qualities, claiming that too often she went to extremes: "I've always been such a bleeding heart. I can't stand to see anyone in pain."

It was true that Margaret's compassion had sometimes compromised her judgment, particularly with regard to men. In Margaret's words, she had a tendency to "always pick the same kind of guy—someone who's hurting; then I try to make him better." She understood, even realized at the time, that she was repeating a pattern that had its roots in her desire to heal and change her father. But knowing this was so was not enough to change her behavior. In effect, the patterns of her life continued to revolve around her relationship with her father—but why? "Why do I let him have this much control over me?" Margaret wanted the anger she felt toward her father to be like a knife, cutting him out of her life. But instead, it was like a rope keeping her bound to him.

Just as with her father, Margaret's efforts to "fix" the men in her life inevitably led to frustration and failure. "Eventually I get tired of being the only one who's giving in the relationship, and I break it off."

For Margaret, the effects of childhood trauma were snowballing, and she was reaching the limits of what she could bear: drug and alcohol abuse, failed relationships, chronic mourning over her father, and now the death of her brother.[6] Some of what Margaret described as other problems for her—sleeplessness, irritability, an inability to take pleasure in things she once enjoyed—suggested that her grief, not surprisingly, was mixed with symptoms of depression. Margaret had hit a wall, and she knew it.

Based on everything she had told me, I believed that Margaret would not be helped by further talk alone. But unlike my early career experience with Susan, whom I had failed to help as much as I'd hoped, I believed there was more I could do to help Margaret move forward by working in a different way.

Healing from Trauma

A NUMBER OF techniques for working with trauma have been developed in recent decades, all of which recognize the need to deal with its effects at the physical, experiential level as well as the intellectual. What these techniques have in common is the goal of enabling people not only to *think* about a memory in a different way, but to *experience* the memory in a different way.

The reason goes back to how our bodies "remember" trauma: we can tell ourselves the danger is passed, but our bodies stay on alert, sensitized to any environmental cues that recall the earlier event. Jon Allen calls this phenomenon the 90/10 response: something happens in the present, but the magnitude of the response to it suggests that most of what you're feeling (say, 90 percent) is left over from an earlier experience. It could be a sound, a smell, a gesture—the tone of someone's voice or feel of his or her hand—but suddenly, you find yourself reacting in a way that makes no sense given the immediate situation. Feelings of fear, anger, shame, the urge to flee or to strike out, seem to come from nowhere.

Like many other clinicians looking for effective therapeutic approaches to working with trauma, I have increasingly turned to techniques variously described as "alternative" or "mind-body" therapies. The underlying premise of these methods is that many of the thoughts and feelings that are part of experience, particularly traumatic experience, are accessible by pathways other than the conscious, rational mind, and some in fact may not be available to the conscious mind at all. So tapping into the information stored in deeper levels of consciousness and communicated directly to the body may be the best way, or the *only* way, to access and process this information. Used along with traditional talk therapy, these techniques help people harness all of their internal resources for healing.[7]

HYPNOSIS

One technique that has seen resurgence in recent years is hypnosis. In a clinical setting, hypnosis is used to help people who want to change patterns of thought or behavior that detract from their quality of life: constant self-criticism, crippling phobias, self-destructive habits. Sometimes these patterns are the result of trauma.

The process essentially involves giving a person simple instructions to "relax and get comfortable," deepening this state with a stream of gentle suggestions, and then either directly or through metaphor addressing the problematic belief or behavior. So, for example, a direct approach to helping someone who berates herself whenever she makes a mistake could include the suggestion that it's OK to make mistakes; a metaphorical approach might include telling a story about how many errors famous athletes make, or how many precautions mountain climbers take to protect themselves in case they slip, because "everybody makes mistakes sometimes." Hypnosis can also allow a person to construct a "conversation" with someone who has died. While a person could be encouraged to do this without hypnosis, the deeper, more relaxed state that hypnosis generates seems to provide for a more deeply felt experience, an experience that can create a genuine shift in how people think and feel about the relationship and about themselves. Hypnosis is particularly useful for helping people become more aware of their own untapped internal resources: their inner strength, their inner wisdom.[8] Hypnosis has enabled many people who felt overwhelmed and helpless to shift their focus from their problems to their strengths.

IMAGERY

If you have ever pictured yourself at the end of a long day sinking into a warm bath, or gone back in your mind to a treasured vacation, you know about the power of imagery. Recalling the sight and smell of the ocean, remembering the feeling of the sand under your feet, really can help take you away from the drudgery or discomfort of the moment (though admittedly not as far away as you might like). Imagery is a way to use your mind to relieve stress, to ease the pain of difficult memories, to soothe yourself when you feel burdened by grief. The images can be spontaneous or structured: detailed images introduced by a professional guide. These are designed to engage the senses—vision, taste, hearing, touch—to relieve or manage emotional or physical pain. Like hypnosis, imagery can be used to access internal resources. For example, someone might imagine a time in the past when he or she felt strong and confident; or a person might take an imaginary trip into the future to a time when he or she has overcome a particular problem, a time when he or she feels more at peace.

EMDR

The technique I proposed to Margaret is a relatively new treatment approach known as EMDR, which was developed specifically to help people recover from the effects of trauma. In the mid-1980s, Dr. Francine Shapiro began conducting research with traumatized individuals that combined elements of existing therapies with something new, the use of alternating stimulation (back and forth eye movement; tapping on alternate knees; sounds that alternate from one ear to the other) to help activate internal healing. In Shapiro's model, traumatic memories are stored in the nervous system in an unprocessed form, with all of the emotions, thoughts, and body sensations intact, ready to be activated by any of a number of stimuli somehow connected with the event. Within the safety of a supportive therapeutic relationship, EMDR brings these memories back into full consciousness so they can be connected with existing strengths and internal resources.

Shapiro's early results suggested that EMDR could reduce the pain associated with traumatic memories and produce a shift in self perception from negatively held beliefs (I'm weak; I'm helpless) to a more realistic, more balanced view (I'm safe now; I did the best I could).[9] In the years since Shapiro first introduced it, the effectiveness of EMDR has been confirmed by clinical trials and thousands of hours of clinical experience. Its primary use remains the treatment of post-traumatic stress disorder, but EMDR has also been used to help people with a variety of other problems, including phobias, anxiety, and grief.

Why does EMDR work? According to Shapiro, the eye movements or other bilateral stimulation, along with the structured retrieval of the thoughts, feelings, and body sensations left over from the original experience, serve to connect the memory of these experiences with the context they lack. The memory is not erased, but it does not provoke the same highly charged emotional response. Typically, after processing a memory with EMDR, people will say, "I can still see in my mind what happened, but it just doesn't bother me the way it used to." As of this writing, there is no simple or universally accepted explanation of precisely *how* EMDR alleviates the effects of trauma. There is, however, a large and growing body of research and clinical evidence to support its effectiveness.[10]

EMDR, hypnosis, and imagery are but three of the numerous therapies available for treating trauma and other, lesser, affronts to the psyche. No one treatment is right for everyone, and anyone who works with trauma needs to be able to tailor a treatment to the person who has come to them for help.[11]

MARGARET, CONTINUED

In the weeks following our initial meeting, Margaret and I talked about her ongoing grief for both her father and brother and the possible impact of her early abuse. We talked about how Chris's recent death had brought back memories of her childhood and left her feeling more than ever like she was alone in the world.

Margaret was open to the idea that her grief was compounded by the trauma of what she had experienced as a child. We talked about why knowing in her head that she was not to blame for Chris's death was not the same as *feeling* different about what had happened; why understanding intellectually that she never could have or would win her father's love was not the same as knowing it in her heart.

The following week Margaret brought me a note with the following lines:

> I could break free from the wood of a coffin;
> But nothing's as hard as getting free from places I've
> already been.

All memories take us back to other times, other feelings. But some experiences are so deeply etched in our minds that we are drawn back to them irresistibly, without warning, seemingly against our will. This is the essential nature of trauma and of traumatic memory. Early trauma creates a past full of sorrow and fear, a place you don't want to live, but a place from which it can be hard to escape.

Several of Margaret's memories seemed particularly painful and emotionally charged, and when I suggested we approach some of these through EMDR, she was receptive. I explained to her that rather than bringing up the past with the aim of analyzing it, EMDR is about *reexperiencing* the past, desensitizing and reprocessing it, and ultimately internalizing the new version.[12] Because it entails revisiting what may be painful memories, EMDR is not for everyone. I had known Margaret long enough to believe that she was a good candidate for EMDR and that it could help her develop a different perspective on the events of her childhood.

Of course, someone with a history of trauma is likely to have spent a great deal of time going over old memories and reliving old terror. Many of the people I see have, like Margaret, spent years talking about their painful past. While talking offers some relief, it can also reinforce a person's sense of herself as a victim, someone whose whole life comes down to whatever damage was done to her as a child. Repeating the same sad story year after year is like walking back and forth in the same worn rut. EMDR introduces a new path.

EMDR treatment consists of eight phases, each of which builds on those previous. The first phase is history taking: the client shares background information and the therapist makes an assessment of the appropriateness of EMDR treatment. As part of this assessment the therapist looks at the client's ability to tolerate the strong feelings that can be evoked during treatment.[13] In some cases the therapist may find it necessary, before processing the traumatic memory, to help the client strengthen his or her internal resources for managing these feelings.[14] If the client seems like a good candidate for EMDR, the therapist provides an explanation of traumatic memories and how EMDR processing is done.

The basic structure of an EMDR session involves bringing up the traumatic memory and asking someone to describe the thoughts, feelings, and body sensations it evokes. The person is asked to describe the negative thoughts about him- or herself that the memory brings to mind and then to posit an alternative, more positive thought or explanation. At intervals, the new thought is reinforced through eye movement or other left-right stimulation. At different points throughout the session, the person is asked to assign a number to indicate the level of disturbance evoked by the memory. This measurement is taken again at the end of the session and serves as a way of assessing the effectiveness of the processing. Here's how the process worked with Margaret.

Margaret and I began her first EMDR session by talking in greater detail about her memories of abuse. There were several recurring themes: her father's rage, her sense of helplessness, her terror that he was going to hurt her or her brother; their efforts to please their father, and the inevitable failure of those efforts; the feeling of crushing defeat, the sinking realization that she couldn't do anything right, followed by the vow to try yet again.

The first memory Margaret decided to work on was of a particularly violent episode of her father beating her mother. Margaret remembered hiding in the attic, hearing her mother's screams, terrified that she or her brother would be next. As she held on to the image and the thoughts and feelings it evoked, I encouraged her to continue following my hand with her eyes, and after every series of twenty or so back-and-forth eye movements I asked her to take a deep breath and tell me what had come up for her. While processing this memory, Margaret experienced the feeling she had had at the time of wanting to disappear. Notice how she describes the experience in the present tense:

> I feel helpless and scared. I feel like I could bleed and cry for the whole world. The worst part is the waiting—waiting for him to come up the stairs for me . . .
>
> One of the things my father used to beat me up about was being so gullible, believing whatever anyone told me. When he did that I would imagine I was behind a thick ironclad door. I learned how to shut down.
>
> It was about trusting, being too trusting. All these years later, I still don't feel safe trusting people. I'd like to be able to take more risks with people. The thought of doing that is exciting but also scary. There's so much at stake.

I suggested that perhaps Margaret could experiment with her image of being behind that "ironclad door," and what she came up with was an alternative, more permeable kind of screen, one that allowed her to filter the input she received from other people without completely cutting herself off from them. After a few minutes she said that she was visualizing "layers of protection" that she could use selectively, putting in place different amounts of protection depending on who she was with and how safe she felt. Together, we continued to process the memory. After each set of eye movements, I asked Margaret to "take a breath, let it go, and tell me what comes up for you now." Gradually, the thoughts and feelings Margaret reported began to shift. Toward the end of the session the thought that came up for Margaret was this: "I know there are still going to be times when I want that iron gate. But maybe I don't need it all the time. But it's up to me. When I need to protect myself, I can. When I want to say no to someone, I can."

For Margaret, believing that she could say no when she wanted to was empowering, and it was essential to her being able to say yes. She had to believe in her power to set limits and make choices in relationships, or the prospect of being in one was just too overwhelming.

The following week, Margaret announced that she felt lighter than she had in a long time. She still grieved her brother. She still blamed herself for things she had done, or failed to do. But she was beginning to believe that she could experience her feelings without being held captive by them. The heavy ache in her heart was easing just a bit. She had found a new path and had begun to consider the possibility that her faith in life was born not of a gullible mind, but of a strong and loving heart.

Another memory that Margaret chose to work on through EMDR was one particular example of a common occurrence in Margaret's house: her father wanted something done, and he had a very specific idea of *how* he wanted it done (though he didn't always verbalize these specifics). In his mind, failure to meet his unstated specifications was evidence of willful disobedience or outright stupidity: either way, it was a no-win situation for the unlucky child chosen to "help" dad.

Margaret, then nine, was told to clean up the kitchen, which included organizing piles of mail and bills that had accumulated on the counters. Not knowing what to do with everything and afraid to throw anything out, Margaret did the only thing she could think of, which was to make neat piles.

She felt pretty pleased when she was done and proudly showed her work to her father. Suddenly she was being hit and thrown outside into the cold, where she was to "think about" what she had done. Whatever it was that her father had wanted Margaret to do with those bills, making neat piles clearly hadn't made the grade; once again, she had failed. Recalling this incident, Margaret could feel again her confusion and shame, the desperate attempt to figure out what she could have done differently. She waited outside a long time, freezing and alone, until her father wordlessly opened the door.

In processing this memory, Margaret again began by identifying the thoughts and feelings connected with it: the belief that she couldn't do anything right; the feeling of tightness in her throat and chest. Like many adults who have memories like this one, Margaret had tried to convince herself that what had happened wasn't her fault, and she had succeeded to some extent in coming to believe this. But she still felt that she could be controlled by others, told what to do and how to do it, and subject to punishment if she didn't meet other people's expectations. Margaret felt no ability to set boundaries with other people, particularly men. She was reluctant to enter into a relationship because she felt that once she did, she forfeited herself, her ability to make her own decisions, and most important, her right to say no to any request, to resist any demand.

All these feelings surfaced during EMDR processing, as did her emergent desire to feel safe and in control: "I want to believe that I can choose, that I can say no. But I also want to feel free to say yes—to be able to take more risks with people, to *surrender myself by choice*. It's exciting to think about that. But it's also scary, like I want to run away."[15]

In time, Margaret was able to evaluate her automatic responses and integrate some of the confidence she feels about herself *now* into the memories she has about what happened *then*: "Then, I couldn't say anything to my father, I couldn't put two words together. Now I can speak. Now it's my job to stand up and tell people how to do things. Then I had no control, there was nothing I could do to defend myself. Now, I would do whatever I had to do to protect myself. Of course I felt small and helpless then; I felt small because I *was* small."

Margaret began to separate the truth of her life then from the truth now: "Now, it doesn't have to just be about what somebody else wants. Being in a relationship with someone doesn't have to mean giving up myself. It can also be about what *I* want. I have to do something every day to remind myself that I'm strong now. I can say no. I can trust myself to know when to turn around and leave."

Margaret's evolving sense of herself and her ability to set limits with other people began to spill over into her feelings about relationships. She imagined how she might be different in relating to men if she really could feel confident, strong, and safe: "I would love to feel moment to moment that I'm safe enough . . . that I can walk into a relationship openhearted . . . that it's not so dangerous to get close to someone."

She also learned to recognize when her fear and rage at being hurt as a child were triggered by someone with no desire to hurt her. Her attitude toward the men in her life began to soften. Her focus had shifted from intense feelings of loss to a desire to allow herself the gift of connection to other people, perhaps to one good man in particular. Good, not perfect.

While Margaret was not seeing a psychiatrist during our work together, many people do at some point have a consultation for antidepressant or antianxiety medication, (or continue with medication regimes they had been on prior to their loss). Just as different people are helped by different therapies, some people will benefit most from a combination of therapy and medication. Medication can provide a measure of emotional stability between sessions and can help a person feel up to the task of engaging in the challenging work of confronting old trauma.[16]

I want to be very clear that *it is not necessary or even advisable for everyone who has experienced trauma to reexperience it in order to move forward in his or her life.* If you are a survivor of abuse, neglect, or other trauma, you may want to take a look at one of the many excellent books that have been written for survivors. It is always important to understand how past experiences are affecting our present feelings about ourselves and others, living and dead. It is especially important for trauma survivors. Often when people feel stronger, they choose to continue their exploration of the past with the help of a therapist. Either way, the goal is not to retraumatize yourself, but to feel better.

Rebuilding

FOR SURVIVORS OF abuse, the process of confronting the past, and the full range of their feelings, is more difficult than for most other mourners. Yet, as we have just seen, the quest for understanding—a deep-down understanding that can be *felt* as well as intellectualized—can be assisted by therapeutic techniques that allow trauma victims to reflect back on the past without having it overwhelm them.

Just as special techniques may be necessary to help them feel the full range of their emotions, victims of abuse also are likely to need continuing help as their mourning progresses and they move on to rebuild their lives. People who have been abused may lack the emotional resources and social skills needed to deal with loss. Something as simple as calling a friend when they're feeling lonely may be hard, given their low expectations about other people's desire or ability to comfort them and their underlying feeling of being undeserving of comfort or love. Emotional coping skills that many take for granted simply may not be available to them at all. As mourning proceeds and extends into the process of rebuilding, abuse survivors will need encouragement, support, and some basic training in how to manage their emotions and deal with the stress of loss and the inevitable emotional bumps and bruises that lie ahead.

At times of extreme stress, the ability to manage one's emotions, to recover emotional balance, becomes essential. For those who get the right messages growing up, coping skills are developed gradually through childhood and adolescence. In the right environment, a child learns from a parent or caregiver that even the scariest and most painful of feelings can be alleviated over time, and that support will be there. This experience fosters the development of an emotional fortitude that makes it possible to go on in the face of highly stressful, upsetting events: it helps makes the unbearable bearable. People who have difficulty managing their feelings are more likely than others to become overwhelmed in stressful situations, and perhaps to resort to unhealthy ways of coping, such as using alcohol or drugs to dull their emotions.

This, then, is exactly the dilemma faced by mourners who have been abused or neglected as children. Because of their experience, they have not necessarily developed the emotional muscle they need to be able to tolerate the feelings that are an unavoidable component of grief. But these skills can be learned. While there are many excellent books about how early abuse affects the developing child, I am especially grateful for the work done by Jon Allen and his colleagues, who coined the term *attachment trauma* and whose books I often suggest to my clients.

Problems with Self-Soothing

WHILE PEOPLE TEND to think of someone in mourning as being quietly depressed, many of the people who come to see me after a loss are agitated and anxious: they sit on the edge of their seat, their eyes dart back and forth, and their hands are in constant motion. As they begin to talk, they often break down into sobs. I wait, offer them tissues, and look for some indication that they are able to speak before encouraging them to go on. I know that this may be the first opportunity they've had to tell their story without interruption, without having to worry about how their listener is going to react. It's a simple thing, just listening to someone. But in most cases it's the single most important thing I'll do for them at our first meeting.

I don't expect someone who is mourning the loss of a loved one to sit dry-eyed and tell me about that person's last days on earth. But most people, over time, gradually recover the ability to talk about the person who has died without breaking down, to recover their composure without denying or suppressing their feelings.

Often, when people seem more emotionally fragile than most, this is something they already know about themselves. Sometimes it's the first thing they'll tell me: I'm not the kind of person who can deal with this; I'm a nervous wreck; I can't sit still; I'll never get through this. Then I want to know, what is it about this person, about his or her history and relationships, that generates these feelings? Why is it that what feels difficult for most people feels *impossible* for them?

Amy, a woman in her twenties who came to see me after the sudden death of her sister, was extremely agitated when she first walked in. As we talked about her history, I began to get a sense of why that might be the case. Amy grew up in a home where she was subject to physical punishment, hit and belittled for being afraid of the dark, where nothing she did seemed to be right, and where she and her siblings were often left to fend for themselves. All this was just the beginning. She then went on to describe a series of abusive adult relationships that she had come to understand as a reenactment of what she had experienced as a child, but that knowledge hadn't helped her to change the pattern. Having tried myriad forms of therapy and more medications than she could count, Amy was still plagued by anxiety. She had frequent and debilitating migraine headaches. A good deal of her internal life was spent berating herself for her past failures and her present inadequacies.

Amy was suffering acutely, but she could not even begin to deal with her feelings of loss; each time she thought about her sister, she collapsed into sobs. After a few sessions, we agreed that before she could go any further, we needed to help her get some immediate relief from her anxiety.

I taught Amy a number of self-soothing strategies and exercises that she could use at home, including deep breathing and progressive muscle relaxation (see Chapter 7). I encouraged her to get outside for walks, to do anything that made her feel relaxed and good, whether it was cooking herself a meal or taking a warm bath. I also made her a series of simple relaxation tapes based on our discussions of places and experiences that she found soothing.

These are just a few examples of self-soothing activities. Some, like reading or listening to music, may already be part of a person's routine. Others, like meditation and guided imagery, can be learned. Don't be surprised or discouraged if a particular activity or strategy doesn't work; try something different. Some people, for example, find that closing their eyes and directing their attention inward brings up disturbing thoughts and images and results in even greater anxiety. Some people find it easier to meditate with their eyes open, keeping a soft focus on a candle or other object.

What Amy experienced in the following months was a gradual lessening of her anxiety and increased tolerance for thinking and talking about her sister. Using these and other stabilization techniques, we laid a foundation for approaching the source of her anxiety more directly. First with imagery and then through EMDR, Amy was able to develop a different understanding of the abuse she had suffered and its impact on her sense of self. Over time, she experienced a change in the thoughts, feelings, and sensations evoked by images from the past.

Feelings About Feelings

ANOTHER STUMBLING BLOCK that traumatic attachment creates for many mourners has to do with how they feel about their feelings. We therapists spend a lot of time talking about feelings, and for some the idea of asking people how they *feel* about their *feelings* might seem like just too much. But while feeling sad, or afraid, or angry, or bitter may be hard to bear, what can be even worse is when people label their feelings, and by extension themselves, as bad—or weak, childish, pitiful. People who experienced the trauma of early abuse or neglect are especially prone to be critical of their feelings because, as we've seen, they grew up without any assurance that their feelings were understandable or acceptable; on the contrary, the message many received was that their feelings, along with their thoughts, their actions, their very *being*, were rotten to the core.

For Amy, Margaret, and others I've met who have suffered abuse, one of the hardest messages to accept, to really internalize, is that their feelings are not bad or wrong and do not say anything negative about them. Feelings simply are.

For Margaret, any expression of hope or optimism was labeled "naïve." In Amy's case, any show of sentimentality was branded as "weak." Amy, in fact, had become habituated to self-criticism, repeatedly describing herself as "weak," "stupid," or "a coward." Again and again, I would challenge these self-assessments. I liked Amy, and I wanted her to stop picking on herself.

One day, after she had responded with barely concealed derision to my suggestion that she might not, after all, be "so stupid," I said half jokingly, "You know, Amy, you really are a tough customer!" The following week she came in and told me that initially my statement had made her angry—she felt I wasn't taking her or her problems seriously. But then she had started to think that maybe I was right; maybe she *was* being a tough customer—tough on *herself.* This became a turning point for her, and what had begun as a desire to feel more at peace about her sister's death became a journey toward being more at peace with herself.

Becoming more accepting of feelings is not easy when you've spent a lifetime denying or denigrating them. It helps to have a trusting relationship with someone who can help steer you straight when you start veering off in the direction of exaggerated self-rebuke. This person may be a close friend, a spouse, or a good therapist. The point is to allow others to influence how you see yourself until gradually you are able to see yourself in a gentler light.[17]

Developing a Social Network

NOT EVERYONE NEEDS an expansive group of friends. But there are times in our lives when, no matter how we good we are at taking care of ourselves, we need the support of a trusted friend or family member. This can be a problem for people who have experienced early abuse since experience has made them wary of close contact. The result is that they are deprived of the comfort and reassurance that close relationships can provide. Sometimes a person has spent so many years in social isolation that the very idea of initiating contact with a potential friend or participating in any kind of group activity makes him or her uncomfortable. This was more or less Amy's situation. Amy did not have many friends, and she had very little confidence in her ability to make them. She was unsure about what kinds of social overtures were appropriate, whether she should call someone and ask her to go to a movie, or talk to a neighbor she saw outside. Based on previous experience, Amy was also afraid that if she did get close to people, they would use that closeness to hurt her. Learning how to make contact with other people and to set boundaries in relationships were important parts of Amy's work. Much of this work consisted of talking through specific situations, offering suggestions, and having Amy experiment with different approaches to making contact. It also involved a lot of discussion concerning Amy's assumptions about how other people saw her, and her tendency to assume that they did not approve of her. More than once in our work together, Amy would call me afterward to apologize for something she had said, or for being "too loud" during our session. It was helpful for her to be able to express these feelings to a person who could respond truthfully and who could also, in a supportive way, help her understand how her tendency to assume that others were viewing her in a critical light could cause problems in her relationships with others.

In the months after her sister's death, Amy came to realize the relationships she had with people often mirrored the relationships within her family. She felt that she allowed herself to be bullied, to settle for less than what she wanted out of relationships, to accept the constant criticism of people who were supposed to be her friends. She had grown up afraid of her mother and alienated from her sisters, who seemed to go through life untroubled by their mother's cruelty and neglect. As adults, Amy felt they had taken over their mother's role, treating Amy like an overly dramatic nervous wreck.

Amy often felt uncomfortable in the presence of her family and friends, but she insisted she didn't have the courage to stand up to them and redefine the rules of their relationships: "I've let them treat me this way, and now I don't know how to change it." Of course, being without adequate social support, Amy felt that much more isolated and overwhelmed by the loss of her sister. So to help her deal with this loss, we had to begin to address the deficits in her support network. Some of this took the form of guiding Amy in the development of the skills she needed to set appropriate limits on how other people could speak to her and what demands they could make of her. Little by little Amy began to do this, and it was a revelation that she could stand up to people and let them know what she would accept and what she wouldn't, communicate her reactions and her needs without having to justify them, and gradually develop more satisfying relationships. She became more aware of what she had to offer other people and what she could expect in return. Instead of constantly trying to figure out what she was doing wrong to provoke the criticism of people who were supposed to be her friends, she looked for people who accepted and appreciated her. She began working as a volunteer with elderly people, visiting them in their homes and offering companionship and news of the world. She found that the women she visited were delighted by her company, and seeing herself through their eyes helped her realize her own value: her humor, her generosity, the knowledge she had gained through her travels around the world. She expanded her private tutoring practice but decided she would limit her work to families in which parents and children were committed to working with her and treated her with respect, not as a hired hand brought in to "fix" the child. What these changes amounted to was a shift in Amy's view of who she was and what she was entitled to in her work, in relationships with other people, and in life.

Seeing herself in a different way made a difference in how she thought about her sister and inevitably affected how she evaluated her role in her sister's life. When she began to see herself through a more realistic lens, it was possible for Amy to view that part of her life more clearly and less critically. Having compassion for yourself with regard to events in your life is not a simple matter of saying, "I did the best I could." To really believe it, you have to feel OK about yourself *now* and to understand on a gut level what has prevented you from making this internal shift in the past. For many people, the path to feeling OK about themselves *now* requires that they develop new skills, overcome old self-defeating behaviors and mind-sets, and undo the damage done to them during a time in their lives when they could not protect themselves from the inattention, the neglect, and the abuse of people long gone but not forgotten.

The More Intimate the Relationship, the Deeper the Wound

NO ONE HAS more power to wound us than the people closest to us: parents, our spouse, anyone to whom we are deeply connected. These are the people who know us best, the ones who've gotten past whatever walls of defense we present to most of the world. They're on the inside, close to our hearts, and whatever emotions they elicit in us are magnified by that proximity. We can walk away from an injury inflicted by a stranger; the same injury at the hands of someone close to us is more painful and more lasting.

Whatever we feel about the people to whom we are closest, we feel deeply, and we continue to feel it when the person dies. We seem to have no trouble accepting this when it comes to feelings like love, which we vow will live on forever, even after death. But as we've seen, negative feelings can be just as deep, and they create just as lasting a bond.

Mourning doesn't require you to honor the memory of the person who has died. It doesn't require that you be sad, or sorry. It does require that you remember all that you can, understand all that you can, and find a way to rebuild your life. All of this is not for the person who hurt you: it's for *you*. You owe it to yourself to untangle the ties of your relationship with that person so that you can go on to live the life *you* want to live, to break away from the track laid down by someone else and find your own way.

Every significant journey requires a certain amount of preparation. When we journey back to places that have scared us, the preparations necessary are those that allow us to revisit the past without being at its mercy. To do this we need to call upon all our resources, especially resources that were not available to us at the time. We need to be able to put some emotional distance between ourselves and events in a way that was impossible when they were happening. We can't rewrite history, but we can elaborate, clarify, and bring new perspective to events that scared us and stories that have defined us. We can reclaim parts of ourselves that have been trapped in the rubble of our past. This is how we become whole. This is how we prepare for the next part of the journey.

When Death Is Too Terrible to Remember and Too Vivid to Forget

*Her suicide is seared into my brain . . . an afterimage,
flashing along the optic nerve no matter what other
reality enters my eye.*

—Signe Hammer, *By Her Own Hand*

hat matters most to people in the hours and days after someone dies is simply that the person is *gone*. This in itself is a violation of what we want most to believe: that we never will lose those we love. But when someone's death is sudden, unexpected, or violent, it is not uncommon for a survivor to feel as if the very ground has given way, that the whole world suddenly has become unsafe and unknown. Any close encounter with death is likely to leave us unsteady, unsure of what to do next, and it will take time for this feeling to subside. But when a death takes place under circumstances that are intensely frightening and overwhelming, survivors must recover not only from the loss, but from the aftershocks brought on by the manner in which the death occurred. In other words, along with their grief, someone who is mourning a loss that in itself was terrifying, may also suffer the effects of trauma.

As we saw in Chapter 4, trauma is an experience that involves feelings of terror and helplessness. Trauma shakes us to the core not only because we're overwhelmed in the moment, but because it leaves us feeling unsafe and vulnerable long after the experience has passed. This is why Allen and others describe early abuse and neglect as *traumatic attachment*: the relationship causes damage not only because of the direct harm inflicted, but because being hurt by someone you look to for love and care makes it very hard to feel safe in the world. Similarly, unexpected, violent death leaves us feeling unsafe and out of control. The more sudden, the more violent the death, the more we perceive that it could have been prevented, the more likely it is that mourning will be complicated by symptoms of trauma. These deaths call up our most primal fears about the fragility and unpredictability of life, forcing us to confront the fact that ultimately we cannot guarantee our own safety in the world or keep our loved ones safe from harm.

While it is not always included under the heading of traumatic death, this chapter also will look at death that occurs following debilitating illness, especially when the mourner has spent months or years providing care for the person who has died. Many mourners have told me that they are thankful to have had the opportunity to take care of their loved one at the end of his or her life, but few would deny that seeing that person slowly consumed by disease takes a toll on the caregiver's own physical and mental health.

What Is a Traumatic Death?

YOU MIGHT BE tempted to reply, "What *isn't* a traumatic death?" Isn't every experience of death, particularly the death of someone close to us, inherently traumatic? To be sure, feelings of helplessness and terror are present whenever someone we love is dying. Many of the people who describe to me their loved one's last days and moments talk about being unable to get the pictures out of their minds. They wonder when, if ever, they will be able to get through a day or a night without the intrusion of painful memories. Still, as hard as it is to watch someone you love die, there are some kinds of death that are more terrible than others. When death is sudden and violent, when it is painful and prolonged, it serves not only as a reminder that bad things happen without warning and without reason, but that they can happen to *us*.

There is no escaping the fact that in the first years of this century we, as a nation, have had to live with the loss of our faith in the United States as a safe haven in a world plagued by terrorism and war. We have had to face the reality that nature still has the power to devastate our cities and rip away the lives of our fellow citizens. But as terrible as these events have been, the truth is that most people who are not directly affected by them go on with life as usual. Impact diminishes as distance increases: it's true for hurricanes, for tsunamis, for natural and man-made disasters. The closer you are, the more likely it is that the impact will be lasting and life-altering.

JEANE

Jeane came to see me about six months after the sudden death of her sister Kathryn. Jeane was twenty-two, three years older than her sister. Jeane described Kathryn as a beautiful young woman who was not afraid to be silly, an energetic, creative woman, a dancer, and someone who struggled with severe depression. Kathryn had spent ten years battling her demons, and Jeane had battled along with her. In fact, much of Jeane and Kathryn's lives had been a struggle of one sort or another. Their parents had divorced when they were young girls, and they spent time at both of their parents' homes. Their mother was loving but strict and had little good to say about their father, an artist whose mental illness and chronic unemployment had contributed to the collapse of the marriage. As teenagers, the girls often chose to stay with their father. He seldom told them what to do or when to come home, and for this they were willing to overlook the fact that there rarely was anything in the house for them to eat other than cereal or cookies.

On the day she died, Kathryn had gone to the supermarket with Jeane to get food for dinner. Shortly after returning to their mother's house, Kathryn went upstairs to her old room on the second floor. Worried about her sister's state of mind, Jeane went up to check on her. She knocked and called to Kathryn, who opened the bedroom door for a moment, then shut and locked it. Moments later Kathryn opened and climbed out the bedroom window, briefly held on to the frame, and then let go. At the sound of her mother screaming, Jeane ran down the stairs and out to the driveway to find her sister on the edge of consciousness. After telling her mother to dial 911, Jeane and then her mother proceeded to give Kathryn mouth to mouth resuscitation. Recounting these events, Jeane told me that she had continued her efforts to revive Kathryn even after she no longer felt any response, because she didn't want her mother to realize that Kathryn had died.

This is a terrible story. I doubt many people could hear or read it and not feel *something*—sadness, compassion, maybe anger, maybe incomprehension. Suicide is something most people have a very hard time understanding. To Jeane and her mother, Kathryn's death was not a suicide, but a horrific accident that resulted from Kathryn's desperate attempt to escape some terrifying threat; they believe she was trying to save herself. The tragedy of this death, like so many others, is that there is no way to know what was in the person's mind at the time. For the survivors, it is a death that invariably raises unanswerable questions. For survivors who also witnessed the death, all of the sadness, guilt, and other responses to the loss are set against a backdrop of trauma-induced helplessness and fear.

As we saw in the previous chapter, trauma-related memories are different from other memories. When a relationship was traumatic, the survivor has to work through that trauma as part of mourning his or her loss. Likewise, when death occurs under traumatic circumstances, the effects of the trauma have to be recognized and addressed. Sometimes people are able to do this on their own; often they will benefit from professional help. Not the least benefit of talking to a professional after such a death is that it can give the survivor an opportunity to talk about what happened without having to worry about the impact on the listener. Another benefit is that the mourner can be given information—and, if necessary, treatment—for trauma and its aftereffects. When someone is unable to sleep, when thoughts and images of the death intrude throughout the day, just knowing there's an explanation can bring down a person's level of anxiety. It also can be reassuring to know that if these symptoms persist, help is available.

So to return to the question, isn't every death traumatic? The answer is no. While death is inherently upsetting and painful, some deaths occur under circumstances that are so overwhelming and frightening that they deprive even the strongest person of the ability to function as he or she did before the death. When it comes to the kinds of traumatic events we're talking about here, factors that generally determine how mourning unfolds—such as the quality of the relationship and a person's inherent strengths and vulnerabilities—move to the background. There are some things that few of us could experience and *not* become broken, no matter how strong we are. The sudden, violent death of a loved one certainly falls into this category, particularly if the survivors witnessed the death. Like Jeane, these survivors have to deal not only with their grief, but with memories and feelings that are too terrible to think about but too awful to forget.[1] Of course, it's not only sudden, violent death that can produce these feelings. What makes death traumatic for some people is not that it is sudden, but that it is lingering. Rather than being taken from them in an instant, their loved one is taken one bit at a time, and they must sit by while the person they knew disappears before their eyes. They must witness their loved one's suffering, the disintegration of his or her mind and body, and the daily humiliations that erase all dignity and identity.

Advances in medical technology have offered another chance at life for many people with life-threatening illnesses. These treatments offer hope, but that hope comes at a cost, to the patient and to his or her family. Having the choice between imminent death and painful, debilitating treatments that may save their lives, many choose treatment. Yet anyone who has endured years of treatment, his or her own or someone else's, knows how close to impossible it is to have a life separate from the illness and the requirements of care.

On the practical side, caring for someone with a serious illness takes time, money, and most of all, energy. If someone you love is ill or dying, it can be hard to think about anything else. Anxiety about the course of the illness permeates every moment. Nerves wear thin as people try to manage the complexity of treatment options. More and more the caregiver exists in a state of constant vigilance, waiting for the next crisis, dreading the next request, no matter how simple. Inevitably, people feel guilty about what they are not doing and resentful of others who they believe are not doing their share.

Worst of all for many people is witnessing the continuing decline of their loved one: the transformation from a whole, healthy person to someone they barely recognize, someone who barely recognizes them. Many people who have lived through the long, slow death of a loved one say that their worst memories are of the unremitting deterioration of their loved one's body: the weight loss, the loss of mobility, the loss of control over bodily functions. People don't want to remember their loved ones as they were when they died, but it can be very difficult to put these images out of mind. What happens is that remembering, which is so much a part of mourning, becomes an agonizing ordeal. You don't want to remember, you try not to remember. Sometimes this strategy works. And indeed, most people do eventually find that they are able to put their painful memories of a loved one's illness behind them and remember the good times, see the person in their mind's eye as he or she was when healthy. But for some people, the memories of illness are every bit as impossible to get past as the images described by witnesses of deaths that are sudden and violent.

NORMAN

Norman sat slumped on the couch in my office, giving little indication that he had the energy or the inclination to talk to me about the reason for his appointment. I knew that his mother had died, that she had been ill for much of Norman's childhood, and that as an adult Norman had lived with her and cared for her until her death. Now twenty-four, Norman felt, like many adults whose lives have revolved around caring for a sick parent, that his life no longer had purpose. This feeling persisted, and it made him feel "like a balloon with the air let out." In particular, Norman was concerned because it was becoming hard for him to do the work necessary to finish his training to be a nurse. Norman was almost finished with this process, having worked and studied for years. Without his mother present to see him reach his goal, the journey no longer seemed worth the effort. Norman wondered aloud why he had ever thought he could do it, why he had ever wanted to take care of sick people, when he couldn't even take care of his own mother without "losing it": feeling irritated, exhausted, resentful of her constant demands.

Yet despite how hard it had been, Norman in many ways desperately *missed* caring for his mother. As long as his mother was alive and needed him, he never for a moment had to wonder what was important to him. The knowledge that his mother needed him did more than give Norman a focus: it gave him an identity. Now that his mother was gone, who was he? Norman was sad, he missed his mother, but he was more than bereft—he was *lost*. He barely looked at me, and when he did, the hollow, sorrowful gaze he cast at me seemed to say, what's the point?

I began gently to question Norman about what it had been like to care for his mother. Much of the time it had been gratifying, sometimes it had been hard, and on a few occasions it had been downright terrifying. Norman seemed reluctant to dwell on these events, and I did not press him. He was a long way from trusting that I would be there to support him, and without that trust there was no way he was going to open himself up to such painful memories. People need to move at their own pace, and someone who has just lost the one person who has always been there for him may be reluctant to risk being hurt again. But Norman seemed particularly guarded; he was there, but he wasn't there.

ANNA

In contrast to Norman, Anna was quick to tell me, in no uncertain terms, what had brought her to my office. A well-dressed, soft-spoken woman in her fifties, Anna began our session by declaring that she had killed her mother. No, not deliberately, not violently, but stupidly, through a series of bad decisions that she never would be able to forget or forgive. In Anna's mind, she had made one "fatally wrong" choice after another, and the end result was that her mother was dead.

For the next hour, Anna catalogued the years of medical problems her mother had endured and her own unwavering attention to the requirements of her mother's care. Anna's father had not been in the picture from the time she was a little girl. Her only sibling, a brother, was married with children and had little interest in hearing about their mother's ailments. Anna, although she had moved to another state and established a career and a relationship there, had never faltered in her devotion to her mother, spoke to her every day, and had her come for extended visits. When her mother's condition took a sharp turn for the worse, Anna left her home and her job to care for her.

Three months after Anna relocated, her mother died under circumstances that Anna described in vivid detail: an impossibly frail eighty-two-year old woman in unimaginable pain, drifting in and out of consciousness and struggling to breathe. This was the image that Anna carried with her everywhere, proof to her of her failure to keep her mother safe, to do the right thing. Why hadn't she gotten her mother to the hospital sooner? Why hadn't she pressed the doctor to intervene when her mother began to fail? At the end of our third session, Anna asked despairingly, "Does anyone ever get over something like this? Do you ever stop thinking about how horrible it was? Do you ever stop blaming yourself?" By way of response I told Anna what I have come to believe is true: that most people do get over it and that there are ways to help yourself get over it. I also told her that sometimes there are good reasons to blame yourself, and that it's OK to acknowledge that you made mistakes. What is not OK is making the past into a kind of club you use to beat yourself up. You need to remember the past realistically, and when you do, the good memories come back along with the painful ones. Gradually the picture shifts and becomes more balanced, more complete.

Differences That Matter: How the Circumstances of Death Affect Bereavement

AS WE LEARNED from Jeane, Norman, and Anna, as hard as it is to lose someone you love, it's harder still to be left with frightening, painful memories from which there seem to be no escape. People who write about trauma-related memories often speak of survivors being "frozen in time": even though what happened is in the past, it *feels* like it's happening in the present.

Whether sudden or prolonged, what makes the memories of these experiences so hard to live with is their power to transform how we feel about ourselves and about our world. How can we go on when our deepest fears are confirmed and, instead of being held at a safe mental distance, take root in our gut? How can we live in the world when we feel that the world is not safe, and we are powerless to prevent the worst things from happening? After trauma, the world as we have known it—what Therese Rando calls our old "assumptive world"—no longer makes sense, because the beliefs on which it was based have been shattered. These beliefs have to be revised; the survivor needs to develop a new basis for living in the world and in the process "find meaning or significance in the trauma in order that the remainder of life not be devoid of these qualities."[2]

JEANE: FINDING MEANING AFTER SUDDEN, UNEXPECTED DEATH

Thinking back on my first meeting with Jeane and her account of the last day of her sister's life, I remember being struck by how *normal* it all sounded—right up to when it turned into a nightmare. As she described the events of that day—the plans to make dinner, shopping with her sister for fresh fish and lemon—I had the sense of the pleasant routine of two sisters preparing for an evening at home with their mother and stepfather. As she began to fill in some of the details of life with her sister, I understood how rare this kind of day had been in Jeane's family since the onset of Kathryn's illness. Much more than just a "normal" day, it had been a day to treasure: a precious respite from Kathryn's unpredictable swings from depression to mania and back again. So when her sister went up to her room, Jeane was concerned, but also determined to help Kathryn recover her emotional equilibrium and enjoy the rest of the day. That's not what happened of course. Jeane heard the window opening, and then her mother screaming. Then came the ambulance, the hospital, her mother's disbelief and denial, her own descent into a wordless, numb state to which, months after that terrible day, she still found herself returning.

You don't need to be told that an experience like Jeane's is hard to forget. You can well imagine that Jeane's suffering was a composite of longing and terror—longing for her sister, and the feelings of terror and helplessness brought on by her memories of the circumstances of her sister's death and her own inability to save her. Jeane had told me a terrible story, but for Jeane it was more than a story—it had all the force of present reality. As she told it, she was seeing it and feeling it. This was made all the more clear to me when I suggested at one point that Jeane take a deep breath. Here's what she told me: "I tried to breathe life back into her, but I couldn't. Now, when I get upset I'm supposed to take deep breaths and relax, but *every time I breathe I see her face.*"

Jeane's description of her sister's death had all the elements of trauma, and her description of her current state of functioning suggested that she was still bearing the brunt of its effects. She was afraid to go to sleep because sleep brought on images of Kathryn's death. Exhausted and distracted, she was behind in the work she had to do to complete a graduate degree, and she often called in sick to her job. Every so often, without warning, she would experience a wave of panic and was afraid she was going to pass out. And she was drinking, not for the first time, but more than she had in the past. Jeane had lived with her boyfriend for five years, and drinking had always been a significant part of their recreation. But now, for Jeane, it was more than that. Jeane wasn't drinking to relax, to have fun: she was drinking to deaden her senses. In effect, Jeane alternated between intense reexperience of the trauma and attempts to numb herself in order to bring down her level of anxiety, guilt, and longing. This is a typical pattern of post-traumatic response: your attention is drawn to the memories, you stay there as long as you can stand it, and then you retreat. Staying in bed, avoiding contact with people, avoiding places that would remind you of what happened, is one way to do this; another is to retreat into your head, to find relief in sleep or with the help of drugs or alcohol.

Like many people who eventually seek professional help, Jeane was beginning to worry about herself—her moods, her drinking, her inability to stop thinking about Kathryn's death. I explained to Jeane that what she was dealing with was not only grief but trauma, and we needed to address both. I also was able to reassure her, when she asked the question, that there was an explanation for what she was experiencing and that, no, she was not "going crazy."

So where to start? If someone has experienced a trauma, but the result of the trauma is that he or she has suffered a loss, what takes precedence? The answer depends on the person, the relationship, and the nature of the trauma. Some people (I took Jeane to be one) are so shaken up by what they have witnessed that they cannot begin to grieve in a healthy way until the effects of the trauma have been addressed. Others (Norman, for example) have a deep and pressing need to talk about the person who has died, to find some immediate relief from the feelings they have about the loss before they are able to confront and work through traumatic memories. And often, the process is a continual back-and-forth between working with the trauma and the loss depending on what has bubbled to the surface of consciousness that demands attention.

And so with Jeane, we began fairly soon to focus on her memories of that day and on the thoughts, feelings, and body sensations that were evoked whenever she remembered her sister's death. Using a combination of EMDR and imagery, I directed Jeane's attention to the most upsetting parts of the experience and guided her through the process of integrating new information and new understanding. In the process, Jeane became less focused on her failure to save her sister and more aware of having done all she could do for her, not just that day, but throughout their lives. Along with this recognition came another set of feelings that were less positive—feelings about her biological father and his failure to provide a home in which Jeane or her sister could feel safe and protected. Jeane realized that she had never in her life felt protected and that this feeling of being unsafe, at risk, and out of control had been intensified by the events of that day. As terrible as these events would be for anyone, they were even worse for Jeane because what happened seemed the culmination of all her fears: I'm not safe; I can't keep Kathryn safe; I don't know how to take care of myself.

As I've said, Jeane's memories of her sister's death were vivid and detailed. She spoke without interruption until she began to describe her efforts to resuscitate Kathryn:

> This is the part I can't . . . This is the most physical . . . It was like breathing my air into her body. When it came back it was like I could hear her voice. It was like we were one person . . . But I knew she was dead . . . [and then] it was like a huge part of me died also. It was so literal that part of me died. Part of me died inside me.

This was it then: the most painful of Jeane's memories, the worst part of her experience. Jeane's voice became quieter as she continued, and she seemed somewhat remote, as if she were watching events unfolding in her head. When the paramedics arrived, Jeane's mother rushed to meet them to bring them to Kathryn, and Jeane realized that her mother did not believe her sister was dead. Jeane's sense of isolation came back in a rush: "I felt like I was alone with this reality for half an hour." At the hospital, Jeane's mother became hysterical. In contrast, Jeane became very focused on what had to be done, beginning with calling her father. "It was weird. I felt like: this is my job right now." She went home, chose clothes for her sister to be buried in, and went to sleep in her sister's room, wearing her sister's sweatshirt.

We confirmed the particular image that was worst for Jeane and agreed to begin our EMDR work with this image. Having previously discussed EMDR and how it works, we did a few practice rounds of eye movements, with Jeane visualizing a "safe place" to which she could retreat if the feelings connected with her sister's death became too intense and overwhelming. Encouraging a person to visualize a safe place and to experiment with the comforting feeling of going to that place is one of several procedural elements of EMDR that are designed to provide a sense of control and security.

During processing, Jeane moved through the images, thoughts, and feelings connected with her sister's death. As she described once again sleeping in her sister's bed, Jeane drew in a breath, let it out slowly, and smiled faintly:

> It really felt like my sister was with me in that room. It felt good. Because that night I was feeling like—how am I ever going to go to sleep? I couldn't stop thinking about what happened. I couldn't stop wondering: was it suicide? It seemed important to know *why* she did it. Did she know what she was doing? Now what I'm thinking is that whatever she did, she was not in her right mind. I was just going over in my mind again everything I was thinking when I couldn't go to sleep. I'm remembering something else from that night, that I *did* eventually go to sleep. Something happened . . . it was like my sister came to me and put her hands on my back. I had a vision . . . a circle of light. And then that was it. I went to sleep.
>
> The image I see most often when I think about that day is her coming to the door and saying, "What do you want?" in that angry way, and what I'm thinking now is all the things she *didn't* say: *I'm scared; help me; go away.* I can see it in her eyes, so much fear. She opened the door to me, and then she closed it. I'm so convinced that she was terrified of something and she was trying to escape.

Here I interrupted Jeane's processing to suggest that we spend a moment breathing together while she visualized her safe place. I was going on instinct; it seemed important for Jeane to be able to have another connection to breathing besides the one that haunted her thoughts. Breathing just seemed so basic to me. I couldn't imagine how Jeane could soothe herself if every time she took a deep breath she became retraumatized. This certainly was not the only way I could have gone at this point, but it's the way I went, and it seemed to help. Jeane's breathing became slower and deeper, and she was relieved to see that it was possible for her to feel better by directing her thoughts to her safe place as she breathed.

Often in working with traumatic memories, when the end of the session arrives, the person is still feeling considerable agitation. This is hardly surprising, given the tenacity of traumatic memories. EMDR and other therapeutic techniques are just that, techniques, not magic. At the end of a session like the one with Jeane, I often close with a guided imagery exercise designed to help someone fully reenter the present reality. I ask them to put "anything you don't need or want right now, anything that causes you discomfort, into a container . . . any kind of container you would like to imagine . . . a locked container that can be opened only by you, when you are ready, and from which you can retrieve as much or as little as you want at any given time." The idea is simple, but many people find it helpful. (This exercise is presented in full in Chapter 7.) I used this imagery with Jeane and encouraged her to use it during the week as needed.

When she returned the following week, Jeane reported that she was feeling less stressed and was sleeping better After remembering how isolated and alone she had felt the day Kathryn died, Jeane decided to talk to her mother and compare notes on what each of them remembered about that day. She did this, and found it helpful. Jeane and I continued to meet every week. Over time she stopped having panic attacks. After several false starts, she began attending AA meetings regularly and stopped drinking. She became increasingly determined to come to terms with aspects of her life that no longer were working for her: her job, her relationship with her boyfriend and with her parents. She got a new job and within months received a promotion and a raise. She moved to a comfortable house in a quiet neighborhood and got a dog.

I provide these details because I want you to have a sense of how a person can survive an event as terrible as the one that Jeane experienced. And not only survive, but emerge stronger. Jeane says it best:

> Kathryn's death blew me apart. But at least I get to decide how I want to put the pieces back together. . . . I never would have believed that her death could be the beginning of me making so many changes in my life, in myself. I'm not saying that I wouldn't give anything to have her back, because I would. But I also know that if she hadn't died, I wouldn't be where I am now.

What course would Jeane's grief have taken if she had not worked through the trauma around her sister's death? Would the intrusive images gradually have receded, leaving Jeane to deal with the more lasting pain of losing her sister? We can ponder this question, but the fact is that, faced with someone who is suffering acutely, the desire of any caregiver is to bring down the level of pain. This is one reason that therapists who work with trauma survivors have turned to methods like EMDR and imagery in the many situations where simply *talking* about what has happened does not provide relief and may even intensify a person's discomfort. Certainly no method is going to work for everyone all the time, but we know enough about trauma and trauma treatment to reduce the severity and duration of people's suffering following a traumatic death. For Jeane, what helped was a combination of many things, including our relationship and the opportunity it provided for Jeane to think about her family and the impact of earlier events in her life on her reactions to Kathryn's death. Within the safety of this therapeutic relationship Jeane could revisit events in her life that had led to conclusions about herself that no longer served her. She was able to reassign responsibility to the adults who should rightfully have assumed it. And she was able to stop blaming herself for her sister's death. Ultimately, she was able to do what she would have believed impossible: to find meaning in her sister's death and purpose in her own life.[3]

When something terrible happens in people's lives, it's natural to suppose that whatever symptoms they are exhibiting, whatever self-destructive behaviors they are engaged in, are the product of the event. But often, even the most traumatic events build on or reinforce tendencies that already were present, as was the case with Jeane. An extreme example: after the attacks on the World Trade Center, a man who had made it out alive came to see me. He was having trouble sleeping, he was anxious, and who would expect otherwise? As I soon learned, however, this man had had not one but *two* earlier experiences in which his life had been in jeopardy: being trapped in an automobile after an accident, and waking up in a hotel in the middle of the night to the heat and smell of fire.

Most of the time, earlier trauma is not this dramatic, nor this eerily parallel: being trapped, the smoke, the fire; for this man, the events of 9/11 were not just *evocative* of his earlier experiences, they were in many respects a *repetition* of the experiences. But the point is, he already was conditioned to expect catastrophe at any moment. When 9/11 confirmed what he already believed, his anxiety level shot through the roof. Prior injuries make us more vulnerable to subsequent injuries. Prior losses make it harder for us to deal with subsequent losses. Lingering feelings of guilt, regret, and sorrow from the past compound our pain about the present, and make it harder to believe that we can feel better, that we *deserve* to feel better.

How Traumatic Memories of Illness Interfere with Mourning

UNLIKE THE DEATH of Jeane's sister, the experiences of Norman and Anna may not register immediately as traumatic. But for them, no less than for Jeane, the memories of their loved one's illnesses arise unbidden, bolts of painful emotion that make life all but unlivable. Like all traumatic memories, these have the quality of being *riveting*: when they are present, attention becomes focused on them to the exclusion of other, positive memories, or to anything that may be happening in the moment. These highly charged memories become a persistent drain on the mourner's already depleted energy. To those around him or her, the mourner appears to be in a kind of fog, listless, disengaged, not interested in participating in the world of the living. Norman and Anna's experiences illustrate how traumatic memories of a loved one's illness and death can bring the process of mourning to a halt.

Norman: I Don't Want to Go There

Norman, as I've said, was terribly sad and withdrawn when he came to see me; he had come only because he couldn't stand being so miserable, but he let me know that he didn't see what I, or anyone, could do to help him. People often say this to me. I wouldn't think to disagree with this remark, not just because I can't help everyone, but because when someone is deep in grief, the simple truth is that I can't do the one thing that would make him or her feel better: I can't bring back the person who has died. Norman was concerned that I would push him to get better, that like everyone around him, I would tell him that it was time he started getting back to work, time he stopped spending so much time thinking about his mother. At least on this point, I could offer reassurance. I would not try to convince him to stop grieving. I would not tell him that he was taking too long to grieve and that he would have to find someone else to talk to about his problems. I had the sense that Norman needed to know that it was safe for him to feel the full measure of his sorrow. He needed to know that I would not abandon him in the middle of his sorrowful journey.

Little by little he came to believe that I would not. Over the course of several months we spent a lot of time talking about his mother and their relationship. We talked about her lifelong health problems, Norman's devotion to her care, and his decision to become a nurse. We talked about fear: Norman's fear that he would not be able to do the work required to finish his training, his fear that his life was spinning out of control and that he didn't have the energy or will to get on top of things. Fear also played a big part in Norman's relationships with other people. Opening up to others felt risky. He didn't know how they would react. He couldn't depend on them to stay or remain the same. Rather than offering comfort, relationships just made Norman feel more insecure and unsafe.

The feeling of being out of control became a theme in our sessions. Like a living presence, Norman's fear of being out of control pulled him away from his grief. He couldn't think about his mother without feeling a dizzying sense of being overwhelmed and terrified. And he couldn't get support from friends or from his father because the possibility that they would reject his feelings or become unavailable to him was just too unsettling. Norman and I talked about these feelings and came up with some ideas for taking small steps that felt manageable, such as having dinner with his father. These things helped somewhat, but did not ease Norman's underlying sense that he simply could not control the events in his life or his own reactions to them.

Once Norman had achieved a certain level of trust in our relationship, I turned to EMDR to see if we could get more directly at what was contributing to his thoughts and feelings about his mother's death. I asked him to tell me about another time in his life when he had felt out of control and afraid.[4] After a few moments, Norman told me that he had often felt that way during his mother's illness; but yes, there was one time, one time he particularly remembered, when he had felt this way more intensely than ever. I explained how EMDR worked and my reasoning about why it might help Norman get a grip on his feelings, and he agreed to try it the following week.

What Norman described to me was the memory I introduced in Chapter 1, a memory of his mother becoming detached from reality, forgetting who he was, forgetting where she was, knowing only that she didn't want to be left alone. Norman's father was also at home, but his mother pleaded with Norman not to leave her. Norman was late for work, and he kept trying to get away from his mother, who was crawling across the floor and clinging to his leg as he tried to get out of the room. Eventually he pulled away with such force that he crashed into a glass-paneled door, shattering it and badly injuring his hand. The following is an abridged account of Norman's processing during EMDR.

> She was just so helpless, so afraid. And from then on I never knew when it would happen again. She'd have a breakdown, go in the hospital, and I never knew if she was going to come out, or how she'd be if she did come out.

> I think that must have something to do with why I'm so uncomfortable with people. I'm afraid to let down my shield, because I never know if they're going to "switch" like my mother did, from someone who loved me to someone who's just crazy and doesn't even know who I am.

> I feel like I can't keep my mother safe. I can't keep anyone safe. I can't keep myself safe.

> I was imagining for a moment that my mother came back. For a moment I felt excited and happy, but then I realized she wasn't going to stay. That's pretty much how I feel about every person in my life.

> I'm remembering again how she looked at me, like a zombie. I can't do anything about it. I can't make my mom better. I can't make my mom come back. I'm afraid. I feel it in my chest and

my stomach. She's holding the backs of my ankles. I want to get out of here. I have to get out of here.

This is not the way it's supposed to be. I shouldn't have to be doing this.

I never should have left. I'm weak.

I'm only human. I was so afraid. It's human not to want to feel that kind of fear and pain.

I'm thinking now that I miss her so much. There's so much pain and sadness.

Just now, it was as if she were here, consoling me. I felt a sense of calm, of contentment. Right now, at this moment, I'm thinking that what happened that day really doesn't matter anymore. *What matters is the love.*

I'm thinking that I'm not sad right now. There's nothing for me to be sad about at this.

In the weeks that followed Norman and I continued to talk about his mother, but now the conversation took on a different tone. Increasingly Norman described himself as "surprisingly stress free. . . . I feel more in control of things lately. I feel more normal. For a while there I really felt like I was going crazy." Feeling more in control made it possible for Norman to take risks in other areas of his life. "I've been making more of an effort with my dad. I feel like I can do that now because there isn't as much at stake; if he doesn't want it, it's his loss." Around this time Norman also became involved with a woman he had known from childhood. "I have all this positive energy, and I finally feel like I have a place to put it."

The last thing I want to do here is suggest that there was some kind of magic involved in Norman's adjustment to his mother's death. Norman spent many months working on his relationship with his father, his expectations about relationships with friends, his doubts about himself. He became aware of the ways in which his relationship with his mother, as nurturing and close as it had been, had also isolated him and made him unsure of how to connect with other people. For this reason and others, Norman's mother's death left an enormous hole in his life. Such a loss is hard for anyone to deal with, but Norman was also burdened with memories that at once were unbearable and unshakeable. The energy Norman expended in keeping his feelings about these memories under control was energy that was not available for grieving his mother's death. What's more, as long as he was so intent on not feeling his feelings about those memories, he was unable to access his positive feelings about her, feelings of being loved and nurtured. Confronting these memories freed Norman to feel. This was the real beginning of his mourning and his healing.

Like many people who are mourning, Norman found it helpful to keep a journal, and he periodically brought it in to show me. Here is an excerpt:

> It's been two and a half years since my mother died. I once viewed death as an immovable force that would destroy my world. I learned otherwise. I learned that if one faces each day as if it were the last, there can be no regrets. I learned that each day shared with our loved ones is a precious gift, and that no one is guaranteed a tomorrow. There are days when I still feel like a kid who needs a mom. But if I can take the experiences that I have had and make a difference in other people's lives, then even my pain will serve a purpose. That purpose is the art of caring—the very essence of what it means to be a nurse.

For Norman, the death of his mother was world shattering, no matter that he had been preparing for it for much of his adult life. Like Jeane, he struggled to regain some sense of control, some sense of meaning. Like Jeane, he tried to forgive himself for failures of compassion or errors in judgment. As hard as this was for both of them, it is harder still for people who must make complex medical decisions for their loved ones, decisions no one can make with any certainty of their outcome. How can a son know when it is time to stop cancer treatment? How can a daughter know whether or not to subject her mother to another major surgery?

ANNA: HEROIC MEASURES AND UNRELENTING GUILT

> I feel like I did everything wrong. I took every wrong turn there was to take. I can't stop thinking about the months leading up to her death. And even now, most of the time I'm in this panic, feeling like I've done something wrong. I see her face, how afraid she was. I remember her dying, and I feel in some way that I killed her, because I didn't do anything to stop it.

Many of the people I see after a loss from illness spend the first part of our initial meeting filling me in on the details of treatment, recalling the multiple times they were called upon to make decisions about care, the many disappointments, the final, terrible days. Almost to a person, they question the decisions they made, and how could they not? How exactly is someone like Anna supposed to know whether to agree to have her mother undergo yet another exploratory surgery to look for the cause of her intestinal problems or to try instead to manage her pain with medication? When presented with alternatives of equivalent, immeasurable potential risk and benefit, how is the average person supposed to feel confident that he or she is making the right choice? If, despite his or her best efforts and the best efforts of doctors, the patient dies, how can the caregiver avoid a measure of self-blame? It's no wonder my first reaction to these accounts is often the reaction I expressed to Anna: *What you're telling me is that you were put in an impossible position.*

When I said this to Anna she looked at me with interest, and I took the opportunity to elaborate. I reviewed the details she had shared with me of her mother's condition and her own rationale for deciding, at the time, not to choose what would have been a more aggressive course of treatment. Simply stated, what Anna had been told was that if the condition was left to resolve on its own and the pain treated with medication, there was some risk that the underlying problem could worsen. But surgery on a woman as frail as Anna's mother posed other risks and the possibility that her mother would face a colostemy. I reminded Anna of what she had said earlier in the session: "That was what convinced me. Mom was always so careful with her appearance, so proud. She never wanted anyone but me to know she was ill. She hated the idea of being an invalid. And she told me more than once, 'Promise me you won't let them put a colostomy bag on me. If that's the only way I can live, then I'm done.' "

Of course, it's one thing to point out to a person that under the terrible pressure of having to make a life-and-death decision, she followed the one clear directive she had been given by the person whose life was at stake. It's something else for her to believe in her heart that what she did was the "right" thing, that she shouldn't have ignored this directive, shouldn't have realized at the time that surgery was the way to go, no matter what had been promised, no matter what the outcome. Because after all, doesn't the outcome prove that she did the wrong thing?

Like so many of the feelings people have when they are mourning, guilt like Anna's is not something that simply can be extracted like a splinter. It doesn't help to tell people in this situation that they did the best they could. But talking about what actually happened, helping the person remember realistically the circumstances of the death, recalling what he or she did to ease the loved one's suffering, is often helpful in shifting a person's attention away from the most painful, guilt-producing images. It's helpful, too, to explain that so many people struggle with these kinds of feelings after this type of loss.

During the time I was writing this chapter, Joan Didion published an account of her bereavement after the sudden death of her husband, John Dunne. The title of her memoir, *The Year of Magical Thinking*, describes how many mourners look back upon their reactions to loss. Much of Didion's considerable capacity for collecting and synthesizing information was directed, during the year following her husband's death, to reconstructing the last days of his life, and especially the hours immediately preceding and following his fatal heart attack. Giving order and form to events that are beyond our comprehension makes us feel less helpless; if we can understand what happened, we can at least have some reassurance that given the same set of circumstances in the future, we would be better prepared and more in control of the outcome. But this sense of control comes at a cost. If the cues were there, why didn't we see them then, when it mattered? Why didn't we use the information at hand to make different decisions, smarter decisions? The problem many mourners have as they reconstruct the end of someone's life is that their memories incorporate information they did not have at the time: not only information about outcome, but often, information about the nature of the illness itself. This was part of the problem for Anna, who, in remembering her mother's last hospitalization, blamed herself for not taking into account information that only became apparent after the fact.

When a loss doesn't make sense, we have difficulty absorbing it, difficulty understanding the implications of what has happened, and difficulty in accepting the loss as real. This, too, is implied in the title of Didion's book. As much as Didion's pursuit of the facts regarding her husband's death could be viewed as a brave effort to confront the truth, the actual purpose of her project, as Didion came to realize, was to remain in a comforting state of suspended disbelief. As long as she was involved with understanding how Dunne had died, she didn't have to absorb the full impact of his being gone. She could hold on to the belief that what had happened was reversible and that she might still, if she knew the right thing to do, prevent her husband from dying. This belief drove her decision to agree to an autopsy:

> Whatever else had been in my mind when I determinedly authorized an autopsy, there was also a level of derangement on which I reasoned that an autopsy could show that what had gone wrong was something simple. . . . It could have required only a minor adjustment—a change in medication, say, or the resetting of a pacemaker. In this case, the reasoning went, *they might still be able to fix it.*[5] [emphasis mine]

The possibility that she could alter the course of past events led to other admittedly self-deluding acts. Didion recounts how she could not throw out her husband's shoes, because if he returned he would need shoes. She spent much of her time alone, "to provide the opportunity for him to return. This was the beginning of my year of magical thinking."[6]

Bereft of illusion, how does a mourner finally come to accept the reality of death? This question arises, in one way or another, for everyone who mourns, but it is harder to answer when the nature of the death strains our capacity to comprehend and live in the world. Life is full of wonderful possibility; life is tenuous and unpredictable. Love grounds us; that ground can disappear from under us in an instant. Human beings are capable of great kindness and courage; human beings have an unmatched capacity for violence and cruelty. Life is full of realities that are hard to accept and difficult to bear.

Yet people do bear them, and like Jeane and Norman, they do more than survive: they get stronger. Belleruth Naparsteck, whose work with visual imagery has benefited thousands of trauma survivors, writes of the "gifts in the rubble," the blessings "bought, admittedly, at far too heavy a price" that come to many of those who have "made it to the other side" of trauma.[7] As you might expect, many of these gifts have to do with a heightened sense of what matters most in life; a desire to live life fully and joyfully, to cherish every day, to let go of petty worries and judgments about oneself and others. For many, personal pain becomes the foundation of a deeper compassion for others and an incentive to act on their behalf. Like Jeane, people who have survived terrible personal loss and trauma often look back and feel—reasonably enough—a sense of wonder at their own strength and resilience, and they want to share their strength with others.[8]

What we have seen again and again is that when someone is not healing from loss, the reason often can be understood as a breakdown in his or her ability and willingness to acknowledge some aspect of reality: that the loss has occurred, that the relationship was imperfect or hurtful, that the circumstances of the death were horrifying. In the next chapter, we'll take a look back at what we've learned about how and why grief gets complicated and what is involved in promoting healthy mourning.

CHAPTER 6

Uncomplicating Complicated Grief

Healthy grief hurts, but it does not make us ill.
—George Vaillant, *The Wisdom of the Ego*

Meredith comes into my office and tells me about the end of her mother's life. She can't stop thinking about how her mother suffered, how quickly and utterly she deteriorated. For months she has been obsessively collecting information, hundreds of pages of records, trying to understand what went wrong. As the person her mother chose to make decisions about her care, Meredith blames herself for not doing more to help her, for not preventing her death. Throughout the day she is ambushed by the mental images of her mother as she looked at the end, helpless and scared. She wakes up in the middle of the night shaking and with a terrible sense that she's done something wrong.

Meredith has bouts of panic at work, constantly worries that she won't meet a deadline or won't deliver what her boss wants. We talk. I ask about earlier losses, and she tells how the year before she had to put her beloved dog to sleep. That too felt like her fault. We talk some more, and she remembers other times in her life when she felt like a failure. She remembers how as a child she tried to avoid inciting her mother's anger, and all the times she failed to do so, and how she hid under the table hoping to avoid being hit. We talk about how she never stopped trying to be good enough to win her mother's love. We talk about how children will do that, will never give up trying to be loved by a parent, even a parent who hurts them, how they'll blame themselves rather than their parent. She remembers being very young, the accidental death of a pet, her closest companion, her certainty that what had happened was her fault, the absence of any adult attempt to allay her guilt, of any adult comfort. Each time her questions are the same: How could I be such an idiot? What was I thinking? What's wrong with me?

As sad as she is about losing her mother, Meredith is dealing with much more than the impact of her recent loss. Her mother's death is the latest in a lifetime of experiences, the net effect of which has been to compromise Meredith's faith in herself, her sense of her own goodness, her own value. Early on, bad things happened in Meredith's life, and with the exaggerated sense of her own power characteristic of most children, she believed herself to be the source of all of them. Meredith's recollection of "killing" her first pet was the earliest of these memories, but my guess is that it was not the first time in her life she felt guilty of some terrible wrongdoing or was made to feel responsible for the suffering of others. Already in childhood, Meredith thought of herself as a "bad seed," a source of misery and even death to those closest to her.

Meredith's story is a snapshot of one person's mourning, of grief complicated by an array of personal and interpersonal factors, some having to do with early trauma, some with the nature of her relationship with her mother (abusive in childhood and conflicted in adulthood), some having to do with the final stages of an illness in which Meredith had to assume responsibility for making life-and-death decisions. It would be hard to say which of these factors was *most* important, which one was at the root of Meredith's difficulty in mourning her mother.

That's often the way it is for people with complicated grief, which can make it hard to classify the underlying cause of their problem. Was Meredith's main issue abuse, ambivalence, or trauma? Clearly all came into play at some level. Classification has its place as a way to organize and explain the variety of problems that interfere with mourning, but ultimately it doesn't capture the richness of real life. A person's life consists of layers of experience which his or her mind recalls imperfectly. Thoughts, feelings, and images inevitably are incomplete, retouched, embellished, and often tied to other memories that may or may not relate to them in any apparent, rational way. Grief gets complicated because life is complicated and because we are fragile and complicated beings.

So, like any model of human behavior, models of complicated grief have their limitations, as do models of "normal" grief. People don't mourn in a linear fashion, progressing from step to step. Mourning is often described as a journey, and it is, but it is a journey with many detours, an uncertain path, and a destination that cannot be identified in advance, even under the best of circumstances. That being said, our model of normal grief still has its uses. As often as not, when I talk to the people who come to see me about what grief and mourning are like for most people, they are reassured; they begin to see just how normal their seemingly crazy state of mind actually is. What's more, by representing how people ideally heal from loss, models of the mourning process help us recognize when healing is *not* progressing and the time has come to seek or offer help.

Whatever framework we use to describe healthy mourning—as a series of stages to be worked through or as a set of tasks to be accomplished—its essential characteristic is *movement*. Most people journeying through grief have a sense that although the terrain is difficult and frightening, at least they are moving through it, however slowly and erratically. What they're experiencing is painful, but the nature and intensity of the pain changes from day to day.

For people who get stuck, nothing seems to change. It's as though the death happened yesterday. Time stops, and with it the mourner's involvement in life. The natural healing process that usually can be counted on to bring a person back to some kind of emotional equilibrium is overwhelmed, and the mourner can begin to feel ever less hopeful with the passage of time.

But while we may look for movement as a sign of healing, we also have to keep in mind that anyone who is mourning is likely to feel stuck at one time or another. Losing a loved one is hard. It shakes up our mind and disorients us. Recovery happens in fits and starts. It takes time to find ourselves again. Very few people wake up the day after the funeral and say, "The past is past; time to get on with my life." (Those who do say something like this generally look back and wonder how they ever could have thought it would be that easy.) Most people have to struggle to get their minds around the reality of what has happened, to believe that someone they loved and needed is gone forever. They know it's true, and yet some part of them holds back from really believing it. In this way, they ease themselves toward a truth that hurts too much to take in all at once. It's part of the normal process of mourning, just as realistically remembering the person and recollecting the relationship are part of the process. And so it goes. In time, people come to recognize the full extent of how life will be different and to accommodate those differences. They start to do things for themselves, to reconnect with old friends and make new friends, to fill up some of the emptiness in their hearts.

People whose mourning is complicated are engaged in the same process every mourner goes through, but for some reason, or reasons, they stop and they can't get started again. They try to let go of denial, but they just can't seem to do it. They try to think about the relationship in a realistic and honest way, but something, usually a feeling they can't tolerate—anger, disappointment, guilt—short-circuits the process. They try to remember both the good times and the bad, but feel pulled to one extreme or the other. They try to find their way back to the path that ends with acceptance, but always seem to end up somewhere they don't want to be. Nothing they do helps, and each day that passes only makes them feel more despairing and hopeless and stuck.

When someone walks into my office in pain, my first impulse is to take the pain away. But at the same time, I know that this is not something I can do, and that even if I could, it wouldn't really be helpful to the person. Emotional healing happens not because pain is taken away, but because it is given its due. This makes the work of helping someone who is struggling with grief a bit different from other kinds of therapeutic intervention, where reduction of pain and other symptoms is often the first goal of treatment. The goal in working with people with complicated grief is not to take their pain away, but to *uncomplicate* their mourning, to discover what is preventing them from moving forward and help them get past it so that the natural healing process can resume.

This isn't something that only a therapist can do, and in fact there is only so much that even the best therapist can do. A therapist can help. A friend can help. Groups can help. Family can help. But it is the mourner who must do the healing. In the end, genuine healing can only happen from the inside out.

Getting to the Heart of the Problem

PEOPLE MAY BE stuck in mourning at the point of denial, or of accepting the full range of emotions about the person who is gone, or of rejoining life. They may be stuck because they were overly dependent on their loved one, or because they had an ambivalent relationship, or because they were abused or suffered a trauma. Or, like Meredith, they may be dealing with many of these issues at once. Looking at all the possible permutations, it may seem daunting and difficult to figure out what is keeping a person stuck and how to help. However, looked at from the standpoint of the goal— to identify the block, or blocks, to healing, and work through them—it becomes much clearer how someone with complicated grief can become unstuck. Everyone who is stuck in grief is stuck for a reason; we have to figure out what that reason is.

And even here, there is a simplifying principle at work, an explanation that encompasses all the variety of ways that people's grief gets blocked. People get stuck in grief because there is some truth connected to the death that their mind simply is not able to recognize or accept. It may be the truth of the death itself, the truth of who someone really was and what kind of relationship the person had with the mourner, the truth that the mourner himself is still alive and has a life to live, or any other truth tied to that particular death that the mind for some reason just will not or cannot absorb.[1]

From this standpoint, the process of uncomplicating complicated mourning seems more straightforward. In one respect at least, it's always about the same thing—discovering the truth, understanding it, and dealing with the consequences. If you're thinking something along the lines of "easy to say, hard to do," you're right.

In his perennially popular book *The Road Less Traveled*, psychiatrist M. Scott Peck writes that "mental health is an ongoing process of dedication to reality at all costs."[2] So it is with mourning. Mourning compels us to come to grips with what are without a doubt some of the most difficult realities, the harshest truths, we will ever have to face.

Some of the realities death compels us to confront are uniquely our own: the truth of what we needed and didn't get from someone we loved; the truth of how deeply we were hurt by another person; the truth of our own perceived failings, our own guilt and regrets. Then there are the difficult truths we have in common with others, the things we know but do not really want to believe: the truth that life is finite, that our own life and the lives of everyone we love will come to an end, that we all set sail in leaky boats, whether we choose to think about it or not.

The first and often the most difficult task of mourning is coming to grips with the simple fact that someone who has always been available to us is now forever out of our reach. When a loved one dies, the abstract concept of death suddenly appears before us in all its intensely personal reality: I will never see my husband, or wife, or parent, or child, or friend, or lover again. Once the initial shock wears off and the pain starts to set in, we'll do anything to avoid it: better to be angry, to stay out night after night, to work until we can barely stand up and hope for a dreamless sleep, than to move toward our feelings about what we've lost.

It's no wonder we try to avoid believing, really believing, that someone close to us has died. If there has not been a death, after all, there is no reason to mourn, no reason to face all that has been lost, all the ways that life will be changed forever. We've seen some of the different ways that denial of a death can play out in someone's life. There can be obvious signs that a person has not accepted a loved one's death, such as keeping everything just as it was before the person died or continuing to set a place for him or her at dinner. There also are more subtle forms of denial, such as avoiding people and places that serve as a reminder of the person who is no longer there or withdrawing into a private world where things go on much as they did before.

The strange sense of numbness so many mourners describe following a loved one's death is another form of protection, a temporary insulation from reality. In this cocoon of knowing but not knowing, the mourner can deal with the practical realities of calling family and making funeral arrangements. The shock of loss will come later, maybe days or weeks later, causing the mourner to question how it was that he or she seemed so calm, felt so at peace, and now feels so utterly ripped apart. People repeat over and over, "I can't believe he's gone." And they really can't. And they won't, until their mind is ready. Miriam Greenspan, writing about the death of her infant son, describes the experience of being shattered by grief, which in its earliest phase is "not about moving on but about being broken."

The merciful numbing of shock must wear off and the reality
of death take hold. Grief must sink in. In the alchemy of grief,
going down always precedes coming up.[3]

For those experiencing normal grief, a period of withdrawal
and denial is a necessary respite, a time for reflection. For someone
stuck in this phase of grief, denial is not about mourning at all, but
about a refusal to mourn. Think back to what happened to Rachael.
She came home every day to her empty house, where she routinely
conversed with her deceased parents. She avoided contact with people or places that would remind her of their death. Rachael's lifelong overdependence on her parents made her prone to this type of
reaction, though dependence is by no means the only reason people
get hung up in this first phase of mourning. Remember Jason, who
lost his girlfriend. His issues were very different than Rachael's, but
he too continued to have conversations with his former girlfriend
many months after her death, to cut off other relationships, and to
retreat into his own world. For Rachael, and to a lesser extent for
Jason, denial of death was a way to keep out of their full consciousness the truth that the people they loved and needed were gone.

Rachael's way of coping with her parents' death was not really
so different from what many of us do when we catch a sidelong
glimpse of reality and decide we've seen all we want to see. We may
hear a disturbing fragment of conversation or an item on the news,
but quickly dismiss it, forget it, move on to something else. From the
time we are very young, we learn to run from what scares us. We
run with our bodies, but we also run with our minds. If an emotion is too scary to confront, we find a way to avoid it. On the one
hand, this is a healthy, self-protective impulse, and it can help get us
through difficult times: certainly, dwelling on what is upsetting is not
a desirable or healthy way to live. But sooner or later, if our primary
strategy for coping with feelings is to avoid acknowledging the reality
that prompts them, we're going to get ourselves into trouble, creating
more and more elaborate ruses to shield ourselves from the truth.

That said, it doesn't accomplish much to tell people in Rachael's situation, "Look, your parents are dead, and you have to stop acting as though they aren't." Challenging them in this way would do little more than take away a source of solace that enables them to continue to function, to get up and go to work, to take care of themselves. What would be more helpful would be to guide them toward developing alternative ways of dealing with their fear and loneliness, other ways of responding to the stress of being without someone they loved. Someone in Rachael's situation could call a friend, go to a movie, write in a journal. I'll suggest other coping strategies in the next chapter, but for now what's important to remember is that denial can be a useful short-term strategy, and that some people have a hard time giving it up, even though it may prolong their mourning. When someone like Rachael—someone who generally functions well in the world and is in touch with her own reality—turns away from the reality of a loss, she is doing it to avoid being overwhelmed by painful emotions. We have to respect whatever inner wisdom guides her to do this. Rather than shove someone toward the light of reality, we have to take the time to understand what it is that compels him or her to stay in the dark. While our goal may be for a person to live in the real world, we also have to remember that every effort to deny or repress emotion has at its core the goal of self-protection. Before a person can shed that protection, she has to feel that it is safe to do so. Denial of death may not be the healthiest defense or the most productive way of managing pain, but it is in the end a way of coping, of protecting ourselves from being shattered by the truth.

How, then, do we get beyond denial to that point of realization that is the first step in healing? How do we help someone who has wrapped himself or herself in a comforting blanket and does not want to have it taken away? Slowly. Gently. Before shedding protective denial, a mourner has to have other resources available, other sources of reassurance and comfort, internal and external. At a time when she may be overly focused on her own weaknesses, she must be helped to become aware of her strengths—strengths she has demonstrated at other times in her life, strengths that have lain dormant because they have not been needed. She will need time to learn to think about herself in a different way. As much as we may talk about the importance of expressing emotion, mourning is so much more. Mourning is about the reconstruction of oneself and about reimagining how one can live in the world.

For Rachael, mourning was about finding alternative ways of dealing with her fear and loneliness, becoming more aware of her own strengths and resources, and tapping into a network of social support. Once she had done this, Rachael was able to begin looking at her relationship with her parents and how their loss had affected her. She began to see her parents in a more realistic light, and she came to the conclusion that although her parents had truly loved her, they also had raised her in a way that kept her dependent on them and ill prepared for their death. Surviving their loss had been wrenchingly hard, but she had done it, and she knew that she could go on. Her enthusiasm for life returned, and she started spending more time traveling and being with friends. She decided that it was time for her to finally define for herself who she was and what was best for her, to develop a new identity, of which she would be the chief architect.

The Cost of Attachment: Reacting to the Separation

ONCE A MOURNER comes to grips with the fact of a death, that person must face up to the truth of its significance for his or her own life. It is one thing to acknowledge a death, quite another to really believe that you never again will see the person you loved, feel his touch, or hear his voice. The mind tricks us—we believe we've accepted the truth, we're through the worst of it, we can do this: and then suddenly the truth hits us again, harder, and knocks us flat.

There are moments, most unexpectedly, when something
inside me tries to assure me that I don't really mind so much,
not so very much at all. Love is not the whole of a man's life
. . . Come, I shan't do so badly. Then comes a sudden jab of
red hot memory and all this "common sense" vanishes like an
ant in the mouth of a furnace.

—C. S. Lewis, A Grief Observed[4]

It is one day since a loved one has been gone, and then two,
and then a week, and then two weeks. With each day that passes,
the fact of death hits home in a different way. Today, it is the empty
seat at breakfast, tomorrow the silence when you come home from
work. The quiet in the evening. The difficulty remembering what
it is you're supposed to do, the yet greater difficulty of convincing
yourself any of it is worth doing, even if you had the energy to do
it, which you don't. We know it, but until we have to live it we
don't really believe it; when we lose what we have loved, it hurts
like hell.

As with other parts of mourning, reacting to separation is not
something that happens all at once. It's a dance of one step forward,
one step back. By this point, the mourner realizes that the only
way through grief is forward, but still is hesitant to move in the
direction of fear and pain. When I'm talking to someone at this
point in mourning I invariably think of the little sandpipers that
run down to the ocean, only to scoot back up the beach every time
a wave washes up, and then bravely make their way back down to
the waterline again. Up and down with the flow of the waves. I
can't help but feel a kinship with those birds. It's not easy to plunge
in, and maybe it's not wise, either. You could be picked up by the
current and carried away from all that you know.

Still, to move through grief we have to do more than get our
feet wet. We have to immerse ourselves, take the chance of being
taken far from the place that has been our place of security and

comfort, a place that is no longer what it was. We can't pretend that nothing has changed, because essential things have changed. Avoiding this knowledge, this truth, takes a lot of mental energy—energy that is not available for healing. Sometimes to go forward, we have to be willing to move through a range of intense emotions: sadness, anguish, and sometimes anger and guilt.

Think about Jeane, who couldn't take a deep breath without being brought back to those terrible moments when she tried to breathe life back into her sister. For Jeane, there was no problem accepting the reality of Kathryn's death. If anything, the images of her death were so vivid and intrusive that they made it hard for Jeane to think about anything else. Jeane's problem was with reacting to the loss; she was having trouble facing her feelings about losing Kathryn because the manner in which she died was so shocking and unexpected. Jeane's sadness and longing were buried in the rubble of traumatic memory: she was shaken, confused, and numb. Jeane continued to relive Kathryn's death, but not in any way that brought her closer to coming to terms with it.

Not every death is as frightening and traumatic for its survivors as the death of Jeane's sister was for her. For most people, sadness gradually settles in and makes a home in their hearts. But for anyone who loses a loved one, there will be pain, and the likelihood is that a mourner will make some kind of effort to avoid it. Children do this openly; talk to a child about a painful situation, and within a few minutes he will change the subject. Adults, too, will attempt to avoid being touched by their sadness. They may try to rationalize the death ("he was very old"; "she was in pain"; "it was all for the best") or even downplay the relationship ("my mother and I were never really that close").

Because we think it will help them move on, we often tell people to cry, because if they "let it out" they'll feel better. Sometimes they do. Sometimes they just feel empty and spent. Crying can indeed be a release, but it hurts, too. People are afraid that once they start, they won't be able to stop, and that their heart, which they have been holding together by sheer force of will, will crack and break. They need to know that they're not alone. They need to know that someone is listening and that we understand how frightening their pain can be. Only then can we begin to speak of pain as a natural part of the healing process, something we human beings are built to survive.

But whatever we do, and whatever the nature of someone's loss, we have to understand that grief itself is something for which there is no cure, because it isn't a pathology. Grief is an unavoidable consequence of the loss of connection. In the absence of circumstances like those we've been talking about—a highly dependent or conflicted relationship, a traumatic death—people generally do not remain in intense grief for months and years on end. But neither does their grief disappear entirely, as anyone who has mourned knows. Years after a death, a person can have a powerful surge of grief. Maybe it's an anniversary or birthday, maybe it's a special family occasion, a graduation or a wedding. Or it can be something as simple, but as powerfully evocative of someone we've loved, as the smell of a particular perfume or the arrival of spring. We remember, and maybe we feel a stab of pain; but it's a pain mixed with the comfort of realizing we haven't forgotten what we loved about someone who has died, and that we never will. For increasingly long stretches of the time, people move through their lives and are not preoccupied by memories of someone they've lost. But for someone who is stuck in mourning, grief remains close at hand. There's no feeling that a gradual recovery is taking place, no sense of resolution or adjustment. Something is wrong. But what?

All That He Was: Taking a Realistic Look at the Past

REALISTICALLY REMEMBERING WHO someone was and recalling the actual quality of the mourner's relationship with that person might seem like a simple thing. It is not. Most people who mourn have a hard time acknowledging one feeling or another, whether it's a negative feeling they think they shouldn't have, like resentment or anger, or a positive feeling they think they shouldn't have, like relief. Usually, the passage of time and the reassurances of friends and family are enough to bring them to accept that their feelings are understandable, part of being human. But for others, particularly people who are mourning an ambivalent or abusive relationship, it doesn't always happen that way. Whatever feelings they're avoiding are too unsettling to let into the picture. They will not admit even to themselves that these feelings are present, and they certainly aren't about to express them to anyone else. They have a story, and they're sticking to it.

Remember Michael, who described his father at first as "everything a husband and father should be." Only with time did Michael remember that he also had experienced his father as demanding, unyielding, and emotionally unavailable.

Or Suzanne, whose mother rarely showed affection and often complained bitterly about Suzanne's failures as a daughter. This was the same woman who sent Suzanne affectionate birthday cards and fussed over her grandchildren.

Or Margaret, who referred to her abusive father as "the devil" but continued to believe that if only she'd tried just a little harder, he might have loved and understood her.

The first story I hear is often the story people have pulled together to bring some kind of order to the chaos of their grief. In the first days and weeks, it is like a snapshot they carry to remind themselves of why they feel so disconnected and lost. With time, this simple picture needs to be filled in, and the more subtle shades of the person, and the relationship, added. We've seen how hard this can be, and we've also seen how people's efforts to avoid unacceptable or unpleasant feelings interfere with healing. Whether it's a desire to see one's father as consistently decisive and strong, like Michael, or to avoid acknowledging a husband's irresponsibility and the anger it provokes, like Barbara, healing just cannot progress as it should until the full picture comes into view.

Whenever we step out of the present and look back, there's a chance that we won't like some of what we see. When that happens after someone dies, it can be a very frustrating experience, given that there is absolutely nothing we can do about it. There is also the chance that something we see will scare us or remind us of how scared we once were. No matter how much we have achieved, it can still be painful to remember how vulnerable we once were and how other people failed to protect us from harm. As a little girl, Margaret felt she had no control over what happened to her. No matter how careful she was, or what she said, her father would continue to behave just as horribly as he always had. This was the truth of Margaret's situation then, and part of Margaret believed that it still was, that she was still at the mercy of forces beyond her control. And yet, when she brought that fear into the light, what also shone through was her own great strength and compassion. She was able to see in herself all the qualities of the woman she had become and to bring together her adult self with the child parts of her psyche that still needed to be soothed and protected.

More often than not, the things we fear turn out to be not quite what we thought. Michael, after facing down the fear of his own inadequacy, was able to understand that some of the very traits he had seen as a sign of failure, like his willingness to show and share his emotions, were in fact part of what made him such a loving and compassionate husband and parent. And Jason, after finally bringing himself to accept that Delia in fact had turned away from him months before her death, was then able to write a new script for himself as a sensitive young man who had known love and was worthy of knowing love again.

The risk a person runs in denying some parts of the story of who a loved one was, or what they had together, is that this story is the foundation on which a person will build the rest of his or her life moving forward. If the story is flawed in fundamental ways, the life the person attempts to build on it is likely to be flawed as well. Many of the patterns and problems that emerged in mourning are likely to be carried forward to emerge again and again throughout that person's life.

We've seen how this happens and what the consequences can be. If we misrepresent in our minds a person who was central to our life, we are likely to misrepresent ourselves. If we exaggerate this person's power, or his or her strengths, we are likely to underestimate or disregard our own accomplishments and potential for independence. If we make the person bigger than life, we will tend to suffer by comparison.

Granted, sometimes understanding is not enough, particularly where past trauma is involved. Margaret well understood that her father's abuse made her averse to intimacy, but understanding that alone did not make her more open to close relationships. That's why techniques like EMDR have been developed, to help people understand both on a cognitive level and on an emotional level that some of the mind's truths do not have to hold the power we give them over us.

If we are to establish a new relationship in our mind with someone who has died, it needs to be a relationship with the person as he or she actually was. Only then can we make sense of our feelings about the person and about ourselves. Only then do we have the information we need to better understand ourselves and our potential, information that we will need as we form new relationships and face new challenges.

Relinquishing Old Attachments and Beliefs

LIKE MANY ADULTS who lost a parent early in life, I have a hard time letting go of things. I become attached to articles of clothing, books, letters, anything that elicits a memory or makes me feel connected to someone who is no longer in my life. Needless to say, this propensity to hang on to things makes for a certain amount of clutter, and so I periodically make attempts to purge items that I feel I can dispose of without provoking a Proustian tidal wave of sensory experience and emotion.

Many of the people who come to see me have a great deal of difficulty deciding what to do with all the "stuff" their loved one has left behind—houses full of furniture, clothes, all still redolent of the smell, the touch of their loved one. When we've lost someone we love, taking apart that person's home, selling his or her belongings, can feel like sacrilege. I think I understand why the Egyptians buried their dead with many of their household objects; it somehow seems wrong, when someone has died, simply to throw out the objects that once comprised a life. More than once, I've heard, "It's just stuff, I know, but it's *hers*."

Emptying out the house of someone who has died is one of the many experiences through which a mourner begins to turn away from the past and toward the future. People vary in the amount of time they need before they can feel up to the task. I have known people who took two years emptying out a parent's home, women whose husbands died long ago who still keep the bedroom closet full of his clothes. People tend to hold on any way they can—whether that means avoiding seeing a loved one's belongings or surrounding oneself with them. Both are ways of coping, of trying to do whatever we can to lessen the pain and confusion of grief.

The downside is that holding on to all this stuff, however rich with memory, leaves little room for new stuff—just as a mind consumed with a life that no longer is has little attention to devote to the task of building a new life.

Metaphorically, and often physically, the time comes to clear things out, to make space in our closets, living rooms, and most of all our minds and hearts, for a new life. That doesn't mean we don't hold on to special memories, our keepsakes. It just means that we move on, because our life *is* moving on one way or another. We can move with it or risk becoming living exhibits in a museum of our own past.

The main reason people do not relinquish their attachment to someone who has died is that they don't want to, whether out of love, fear, obligation, guilt, or any number of emotions. They may feel, like Rachael, that it's a kind of abandonment or betrayal. Or like Jason, that they will never replace what they've lost. Or like Margaret, that if they replay things enough times in their mind they just might have a different outcome.

What each of these people came to understand, and what everyone who goes through the mourning process ultimately comes to understand, is that giving up the relationship that was does not mean giving up a connection to the person who has died. In fact, only by accepting the past as past, and relinquishing what was, does it become possible to establish a new connection with the person you loved, a connection that can live comfortably in your heart and mind without turmoil.

Human attachments are as varied as the hopes, dreams, and plans people share, as diverse as the responsibilities and roles they fulfill for one another. It's no simple matter to define who a person was, what he or she meant to us, and who we are without that person. We seldom become aware of all that our connection to someone means to us until that connection is broken. When that happens, we have a choice: to continue to look to the past in hopes of changing what can no longer be changed, or to do our best to seek the truth of what was, make a place for it in our hearts, and find new paths to fulfillment. Once again: easy to say, hard to do. But you don't have to do it all at once. And you don't have to do it alone.

Who Am I Now? Moving into the New World Without Forgetting the Old

MOST PEOPLE WHO seek help when they are grieving do so not because they want to disconnect from their lost loved ones, but because they want to feel like themselves again, and they've come to fear that that may never happen. Yet often, when they do begin to feel like themselves, when they have a "good day" or a good week, they worry that their connection with the person who has died is fading away, that now, truly, their loved one is becoming lost to them. The result is that a person can feel bad when she feels bad, and also feel bad when she feels good: not a state of mind that encourages readjustment and adaptation.

It's not unusual to feel ambivalent about feeling better, especially if you believe that reentry into the world means that you are leaving your loved one behind. You are not. If you think about it, really, how could you? The truth, and I say this because I have seen it over and over again, is that it is possible to let go of pain without losing a connection to the person who has died. How that connection will be maintained, how big a part the person will continue to have in your life, depends on many things. There are healthy connections and unhealthy connections, but the line between the two is not always clear, and what looks like healthy adaptation is sometimes grief denied or otherwise delayed.

I remember a brother and sister who came to see me after the death of their mother. Both were clearly grieving, but the sister, to all appearances, was having the harder time. While the brother described the funeral and their plans for putting their mother's house on the market, the sister wept quietly, saying only that her mother was her life, and she didn't know how she was going to live without her. I continued to meet with the sister for several months. She saw friends, but spent a lot of time by herself, responding to letters of condolence, coming straight home from work to eat and go to sleep. Right around the time she was starting to feel more herself, her brother began to fall apart. He had thrown himself back into a hectic social and work schedule. Now, six months later, he was barely able to get out of bed in the morning and had a variety of physical symptoms that made it hard for him to function. His job, which required a great deal of travel, had become more of a burden than a welcome distraction, and he had little desire to go out with people who had "no idea of what it's like to lose a parent." What does it mean to reenter the world when the world as you knew it is gone?[5]

Let's go back to Barbara. Five years after her husband's death, Barbara was still furious about the turn her life had taken. Her beliefs about how the world should be—that husbands take care of wives, that she, in particular, would always have a man to take care of her—had been upended.[6] But rather than reconsidering her beliefs, she had assumed a posture of permanent protest. We know something about why this was: she needed to hold on to her beliefs about the world, her assumption that she would always be taken care of, because she did not believe she could take care of herself.

Over the course of the next several months, Barbara gained a different understanding of her marriage, her husband, and herself. She realized that for all his good qualities, Bob had not been a reliable provider, and she had not been a pampered princess. Barbara had always worked, and at times hers was the only income the family had. Since Bob's death Barbara had managed to pay her mortgage and raise her children. Looking back at what she had come through and what she had accomplished, Barbara began to think about herself in a different way, to revise the story she had been carrying in her head—the story about the poor widow, the abandoned little girl. Yes, she was on her own, but that was OK, she could handle it. Of course, all of this took time, not to mention a lot of courage on Barbara's part. Change produces anxiety. A person in Barbara's position needs support, encouragement, and sometimes concrete assistance in learning how to manage new responsibilities and new roles. For example, even as Barbara became more self-confident and less afraid, she continued to pay her bills late, forgot to schedule needed repairs on her house, and often declared herself helpless and overwhelmed. She had setbacks and then moved forward again. At these times, it became important to do more than comfort and console; what Barbara needed was to be gently encouraged to accept her new reality and to change along with the changes in her life.

And Barbara did change. She got down to business with a financial planner. A year after her children were out of the house, she decided to sell it and move to a smaller place that was more affordable. These changes were particularly significant for Barbara because they demonstrated that she was adopting new ways of being in the world.[7] Rather than waiting for Bob to come back and take care of things, or for another man to come and rescue her, she was taking matters into her own hands.

The result of these changes was that Barbara was able to live in the real and present world rather than being constantly frustrated and angry about not being able to return to the world as it was. She continued to miss Bob, and in fact she began to tell me more about positive qualities in him that had nothing to do with taking care of her—his sense of adventure, his humor, his loyalty to friends. At the same time, her own identity continued to evolve. She rediscovered old passions and explored new paths. Years before she had loved to dance, and now she found she still loved it. She began thinking about transitioning out of her agency social work job and building a private practice focused on helping other women facing changes in their lives. In short, Barbara made the decision to give up parts of her identify that were no longer working for her and beliefs that no longer served her. She took a hard look at the past and revised the story of her marriage so that it was less idealized and more real. In so doing, she did not lose her connection to Bob. If anything, she was better able to remember the man he truly was—to remember fully why she had loved him, and to know that she always would. And she was ready to discover what else the world had in store for her.

The Present Moment: Reinvesting

I AM THINKING as I write this that for many readers the idea of reinvesting in life after losing a loved one may seem a distant possibility and, despite all I have said, a betrayal—especially if reinvesting involves forming new attachments. I can only say that in my experience, people who know how to love, and who have loved deeply, have the capacity, and with time the desire, to love again. Whether and if they do depends on many things, not the least being their ability to secure a peaceful place to hold the love they still have, and always will have, for the one who is gone.

Reinvestment is not just about relationships. It may be about moving from the home you shared for forty years to a new home, maybe in a new place. It's about pursuing new dreams, new ambitions, that have to do with life now and in the future.

As we've seen, there are many reasons that mourning can bog down, some involving the nature of the relationship, others the nature of the death. We can understand complicated grief as being rooted in a person's early history, parenting, connections with other people, or like Meredith, maybe all of these at once. Given the underlying complexity of the problems that people can face when they are grieving, it would be unreasonable to suggest a simple strategy for healing from complicated grief. Still, there are ways to help yourself, some of which have been mentioned in the stories you've been reading. I'll describe some of these more fully in the next chapter. Under some circumstances, it may not be advisable, or even possible, for a person who is having difficulty after a loss to address problems without professional support. Part of helping yourself is knowing when to ask for help from others, and that too is something we'll address.

CHAPTER 7

Paths Toward Healing

*You cannot keep the birds of sorrow from flying overhead, but
you can prevent them from building nests in your hair.*
—Chinese proverb

*W*hat does it mean to *heal* from grief? What
does it feel like, and how long does it take? The
experience of losing someone close to you evokes
powerful feelings and can raise difficult questions. At some point,
almost everyone confronted with loss wants to know, Why am
I having such a hard time? Will I ever get over this? While the
particulars differ, every loss of a loved one is painful, often much
more painful, disorienting, and enduring than people expect. The
simple truth is that we can never anticipate what it will actually
feel like when someone we love dies, and consequently we cannot
fully prepare for the loss. We can learn to cope with loss only after
it has happened, as we go along day by day. As the proverb at the
beginning of this chapter suggests, things will happen that are out
of our control. But we can take steps to contain the damage they
inflict, and in so doing we can preserve our desire and capacity to
go on with life.

I began writing this book because I wanted to share some of
what I've learned about grief, about how people heal after a loss, and

how they don't. One of the things I've learned is that some of the most effective ways of helping people are also the simplest: listening to people's stories without judgment, bearing witness to their pain, not with pity for what they have suffered but with respect for what they have survived. I've learned that most people, not just a heroic few, have within them reserves of strength and levels of emotional depth that have been waiting, untapped, until they are called upon to cope with experiences that are beyond anything they have encountered before.[1] I've learned that seeking the truth is an essential part of healing emotional wounds, loss among them, and that deep down people are driven by a powerful desire to find the truth and confront it, difficult as it may be.

If you think you may be suffering from complicated grief—if you think you're stuck—it may be that some of the stories and ideas in this book will strike a chord and help you get unstuck. Reading is one way to come to a better understanding of how you have come to a given point in life. Reading about how others have faced difficulties in their lives can get you thinking about what you might do to move in a new direction, or it may motivate you to seek additional help if that's what you need. There are other things you can do to help yourself as well.

This chapter is a little different from those before it. It speaks directly to someone who has suffered a loss, though it also can be a guide for those who want to help others they know who may be suffering. It's more like a conversation I might have with someone in my office, except that if you were in my office, I would be speaking just to you, about your life and your loss. What I can say here is of necessity more general, so while some of it may remind you of your own situation, other parts may not; some suggestions will strike you as potentially helpful, others won't. Suggestions that may sound like too much today may appeal to you tomorrow, when the initial shock of loss has subsided. All that matters is that you discover what works for you, the particular resources, internal and external, that will help you feel less overwhelmed and more confident in your ability to cope.

Long before there were therapists who specialized in mourning, people mourned. Loved ones died, and people got through it. Over time, religious and communal rituals evolved to help people in mourning. Many of these traditional ways of coping with loss—quiet reflection, creating sacred spaces and rituals of remembrance—are recalled in the practices Greenspan suggests for helping along the "alchemy" of grief, the process by which the mind transforms dark emotions and heals itself.

It's also true that before therapy, people got stuck. And often, with the help of friends and family, they got themselves unstuck. The point is that getting unstuck doesn't necessarily involve a great deal of complex analysis, or a therapist. It doesn't necessarily require an understanding of the ins and outs of the mourning process or the ability to identify precisely where that process has broken down. There are steps people can take on their own, and with the help of friends and family, to heal their grief, and I'm going to talk about some of those things now. At the same time, I believe it's important for people to recognize when they need extra help and know how to find it. Many people are reluctant to seek professional help and only do so when their pain has become unbearable. We'll talk a bit about this as well.

If you were to walk into my office, I'd ask you a few basic questions about yourself, and then I'd ask you to tell me about your loss: how it happened, when, what was hardest for you about dealing with it, and so on. I'm often struck in these early conversations by how hard people can be on themselves when they're grieving. I also see how hard others—even those who are well-meaning—can be on the recently bereaved. People think that the mourner should be past his or her pain, even if the loss occurred only months or even weeks before. This just isn't a reasonable expectation after the loss of a loved one. Feelings that have been part of us for years don't evaporate in a matter of months. Attachments don't disintegrate just because someone has died, and that is a good thing, even though in the early part of grief it may feel like a cruel trick of nature.

I can't tell you what amount of time is "normal" to grieve, but I can tell you that it is longer than most people seem to think it is! It may be a year or more before people take firm steps into a new life, two years before they really begin to feel invested in that life. In a world of digital organizers and multitasking, many of the people I see want me to give them a timeline. They want to know what to expect and when. This is, after all, what much of the rest of our lives is about, or what we'd like to think our lives can be about: planning, anticipating, being proactive. Grief is humbling for the very reason that it cannot be managed like a business or planned like a vacation. You have to give it time. On the other hand, if you've suffered a particularly wrenching loss or experienced a traumatic loss, time may not be enough. You're probably going to need help, and the sooner you get it, the better off you'll be.

Sometimes it's clear that a person's grief will be complicated, but not always. How do you know if you're headed in that direction? The first question to ask yourself has to do with movement, and the second, with how much your grief is interfering with your ability to function—to eat, sleep, work, and to be there for the people in your life. If months have passed and you seem to be facing the same issues, the same feelings, withdrawing from life and those around you, you might want to think about what to do to get yourself moving. Deep down, you probably know if you are making progress or not. If you really don't know if your mourning is progressing, talk to someone who has the knowledge and experience to help you figure it out. At least once a week, I talk to people who have suffered for months or even years because they thought there was nothing else they could do but wait for it to get better, or because they believed it never could get better. I hope you won't let this happen to you. There is no quick or easy way to shed your grief, but there are ways to make it more bearable.

If you think you're stuck, there are things you can do to help yourself. I'll talk about some of these first and then go on to ways to get help from other people, starting with family, friends, and your community. Then I'll talk about various types of professional help that are available and how to find them.

Facing the fact that you are not healing from your loss is in itself a difficult thing. Many people who suffer from complicated grief experience a sense of hopelessness and desperation that can make it very tough for them to find the energy to heal. Whatever problems they are having in coping with loss may be part of a pattern of being overwhelmed by emotionally stressful events that has plagued them throughout life. Add to this the fact that people who are stuck in grief are often trying to shield themselves from thoughts and feelings that are too frightening or upsetting to confront, and it's clear that what we're talking about here is no easy undertaking. So before we go any further in talking about how to get yourself moving, I would ask you to make three commitments to yourself. I base these on the sorts of things I see in my work with people who are grieving, and generally I deal with them as they arise. As we go through them, I hope you'll be able to see why I consider each so important to healing, as important as anything else you might do to get yourself back on track.

The first commitment is that you will be gentle with yourself and others who share your grief. There seems to be no end to the reasons people can find to berate themselves after the loss of someone they loved. It may be the fact that they aren't healing on a self-imposed timeline: "I'm weak. I'm refusing to get better." Or they berate themselves for what they believe are defects in their emotional makeup: "I've always been overly emotional." Or they feel guilty about something having to do with the death: "I should have been by her side at the end"; or about things they may have said or done to the person who died: "I was selfish"; or because of thoughts they've been having since the death: "I shouldn't think bad things about him when he isn't here to defend himself."

Just telling yourself or someone else to "stop being so hard on yourself" seldom does anything to make those feelings go away. So, just as people can always find reasons to berate themselves, here are a few reasons *not* to:

- You will not move forward in your mourning if you keep repeating the same self-critical messages.
- You can make yourself physically sick if you push yourself too hard.
- You risk hurting those who love you by prolonging your own pain.
- You are a human being, and you are no more justified in treating yourself harshly than you would be in treating anyone else that way.
- You may be wrong about yourself. Put another way, just because you have been giving yourself the same negative messages over and over again doesn't necessarily mean that they are true.

The second commitment you need to make is to seek the truth. I really do believe that healthy mourning is about coming to terms with truth: the truth of death, the truth that the person is no longer with you, the truth of who he or she was and the relationship you had together, the truth of how you, and your life, have been changed. None of this is easy even under the best of circumstances. It takes great determination to move toward what you fear. One word about truth, though: it may not be what you think it is. Jason was afraid of the "truth" that he was not worthy of love. But when he finally looked that deeply held belief straight in the face he discovered that it simply wasn't real, that he was in fact as worthy of love as anyone.

That said, I want to be very clear, once again, that some truths are incredibly painful and should not be confronted without support. Before you can start to look at a reality that is frightening to you, whether it is the reality of a painful past or the reality of a traumatic death, you need to be in a place where it is safe to do so. *If you feel overwhelmed at any time in following some of the suggestions I'll offer, just stop what you are doing.* Take a break. Call a friend. If you feel the time has come, seek out someone who can provide the kind of personal, professional support that will help you to move ahead.

Which brings us to the third commitment you need to make: no matter what the circumstances of your loss, or the nature of your grief, you will look to others to help you through this difficult time in your life. Throughout history, mourning rituals have been about family, friends, and community. Mourning simply is not something that we are meant to go through alone. Sadly, we live in a time and place where the ties that once held people together are tenuous for many. But even when it may not be obvious who or where they are, people are available to help you. You have to commit yourself to finding them, and I'll offer some suggestions that will help you know where to look.

Perhaps more than anything else in life, death is something we confront without quite believing in it. It's part of what we all know, and yet in another sense, it is outside of what we can know.

When death is right in front of us, a reality we must confront in this very moment, we use whatever internal resources we can muster to soften the blow, to limit what we absorb so that we're not overwhelmed by fear and pain. Metaphorically, if not literally, we close our eyes. Then slowly, tentatively, we open them and take in a bit more, until something inside us compels us again to retreat. This process of opening up and shutting down is especially evident in children, whose tolerance for thinking and talking about death may be no more than ten or fifteen minutes. It's not hard to know when children have reached their internal limits; they'll change the subject or start bouncing on the couch or running around the room to flush out feelings that are too uncomfortable to sit with. Adults, too, have ways of limiting their dose of difficult feelings, one of which is to alternately move toward, and then away from, the source of their pain. We think about the death, and then we don't think about it. We spend time reflecting on the past, and then we take a break and live in the present. Each time we do this, our ability to deal with a difficult reality is strengthened, much as a muscle is strengthened by working it to exhaustion and then allowing it to recover.

More than ever, we understand now that mourning is not a linear process of recovery, but a process of alternating attention, and of emotional ups and downs. The suggestions that follow are my attempt to support you in the day-to-day, week-to-week ups and downs of your grief, to encourage you to follow the flow of your mourning as it alternates between active grieving and intervals of rest. Taking care of yourself when you're grieving means recognizing that there are times when you need to turn inside, and times when you need to reconnect with the world. In order to heal, you must be able both to remember the past and to believe in the future.

Preparing Your Mind to Move Toward What Hurts

WHEN I WORK with people who are having difficulty recovering from a loss, my goal is not just to help them with their grief, but to do whatever I can to affect the overall ecology of their lives. I encourage them to take in experiences of all kinds that may give comfort—music, poetry, nature. I encourage people to use all of their senses to soothe themselves. I emphasize the importance of self-care, including the need to be mindful and responsive to what-ever it is they are feeling at the moment. I talk about the difficulties that arise when we judge our feelings and the value of recognizing each feeling for what it is: a flare sent up from the deepest regions of the self, a marker for thoughts and emotions that live in the body and the spirit.

For all the reasons we've discussed, being able to recognize and acknowledge truth is essential to healing from grief. This is but one of the many reasons that we need to have periods of quiet reflection, interludes of stillness. The world is a noisy place, and it can be difficult to hear what we need to hear. We're constantly bombarded not just by the noises outside, but by the noises within: relentless transmissions reminding us of all the obligations, responsibilities, and requirements of work, family, and the rest of our lives. So the question arises, how do we find a place of refuge, a quiet place where we can hear our thoughts and feel our feelings? For thousands of years, people have sought the answer to this question by deliberately cultivating mindfulness. Meditation is one, but certainly not the only, such practice. Jon Kabat-Zinn, who has introduced thousands of people to the benefits of meditation, writes that mindfulness is about "waking up" and having an "appreciation for the fullness of each moment we are alive."[2] The cultivation of mindfulness is not a practice separate from life, but a way of living. To live mindfully is to be fully tuned in to your own life, noticing the flow of thoughts through your mind, the feelings in your body, and then expanding your awareness outward into the world to the sounds and sights around you.

Many people tend to think of meditation as an escape. In one sense that can be true, in that just sitting quietly can relieve some of the tension and turmoil they are feeling in their lives. At the same time, tension and turmoil can distract people from what may be their true thoughts and feelings, a way to avoid confronting what our minds and bodies are trying to tell us. (A person may find, for example, that while all of his attention has been taken up with anger at the physician who failed to save his mother's life, all that really matters to him, what's really upsetting him, is that she is gone.) So the point of mindfulness techniques is not relaxation alone, though relaxation can be a good thing. More than simple relaxation, though, the purpose is to prepare your mind to heal, to tune out the unessential and to focus on what is real and true for you.

Often, people's initial attempts with meditation are frustrating: their minds race, they can't stop thinking. It's easy to understand why. The fact is that our minds are racing most of the time—it's just that we're not aware of it until we try to slow down. Meditation and other techniques allow us to become aware of the buzz in our heads, to notice the patterns of our thoughts. The idea is not to make yourself think or feel differently, but simply to *notice* what you're thinking or feeling, without judgment. Again, this is easy to say, hard to do. That's why you have to practice.

You don't need a book on the topic to be more mindful, though if you find you're helped by some of the exercises I'm about to suggest, you might want to look in the Resources section to find a book that goes more deeply into the topic. Mindfulness is not about going off and retreating for months of silent meditation. You can try an exercise right now if you want to. Here's one you can do just about anytime, anywhere.

As Simple as Breathing

NOTICE YOUR BREATHING. In particular, it's worth paying attention to those times when you *stop* breathing and to notice how you feel at that moment. Sometimes, when people are talking to me about something that upsets them, I'll ask them to notice their breathing. They'll realize that it's shallow, or even that they're holding their breath, which is a common response to feeling anxious or afraid. The problem is that when people stop breathing, their mind gets the message that something is wrong, that they're not OK, and their anxiety can escalate. The way to counter this message from the body is to take a long, deep breath. It's good to know that when you're feeling shaky, relief can be as simple as taking a few deep breaths (but not so deep or so fast that you hyperventilate!) and noticing how your body starts to relax.

Taking this one step further, you can practice noticing your breathing to help yourself feel calm *before* something happens to upset you—in other words, you can condition yourself to experience a connection between taking a breath and feeling calm. Then, when you are stressed, it will be even easier and more automatic for you to calm yourself by taking a breath. Here is one version of an exercise for soothing yourself with your breath:[3]

Sit or lie down in a comfortable place. Begin by breathing normally, and then gradually slow your breathing, being conscious as you do so of the deep inhalation and the slow exhalation of breath. As you breathe in, focus all of your attention on your breath. Notice your breath as it enters your abdomen and your chest; feel your abdomen and your chest opening and expanding with your breath. Then, as you exhale, focus all of your attention on the out breath. Take a moment to notice how your body feels, and do it again. Whatever emotions surface as you breathe, notice them and breathe through them (don't fight them, don't judge them, just notice them and let them go as you continue to breathe). Try doing this for five minutes.

Focusing on your breath, noticing and breathing through your feelings, is a way to begin to strengthen your emotional muscle. You're soothing yourself and at the same time having the experience of sitting with yourself, letting your feelings come to the surface, noticing that you can feel a feeling without having it take you over. Noticing your emotions without judging them, being aware of your feelings and releasing them gently instead of shutting down, helps you feel more in control. Instead of avoiding your emotions, you meet them, identify them, hang around with them a bit, and then let them go for the time being.

There are many ways to practice being aware of your feelings. Here's one that I like:

When you wake up in the morning, take a few moments to let your mind sort through the remains of your dreams, breathing slowly as you think about the day ahead. Notice any concerns you have about the day, and take a few moments to think through how you are going to manage them. Throughout the day, notice what you are feeling and think back to that moment when you first woke up. Take the time to breathe in, to acknowledge your feelings without judging or overanalyzing. Just notice, take in what you need to know, and let the rest go.

What I have just described are informal mindfulness practices, things you can incorporate into your day without much thought or preparation. There are also more structured approaches to try, such as a daily practice of sitting meditation. This can be done on your own, with a meditation tape, or you can try a meditation group. Any of these will get you started, and you will know soon enough what works best for you. Many people are coming to appreciate the value of mindfulness practices as a way to increase tolerance for emotion, and also as a way to calm and prepare the mind to move through the journey of mourning.[4]

Inevitably, there will be days when what you most need is simply to nurture yourself, to find some comfort and relief from your sadness. You may already know what's best for you. You may be the kind of person who will run a hot bath, light some candles, and put on some music. Or you may be someone who finds solace in walking, or gardening, or going for a run. Here is another approach to self-soothing that many people who come to see me find helpful. It's all about finding a safe place in your mind.

Think about a place where you feel very comfortable and relaxed. It can be a place you've been to, a place you remember from childhood, a place in your imagination. Sit or lie down in a relaxed position with your eyes closed and bring all of your attention to that place and how it feels to be there. Breathe in the smells, hear the sounds, feel the temperature of the air on your skin. Use all of your senses to bring you to this place where you feel so peaceful, so calm and comfortable. Stay there as long as you like, just enjoying the feelings in your body. Let your mind wander to all the corners of this place, taking it all in. There is nothing else you need to do right now, just to be here.

Putting Aside Troubling Thoughts and Feelings

DO YOU EVER have the sense that your mind is like a cluttered attic, full of junk that you don't need, but can't seem to throw away? Where did all this stuff come from? Do you have to carry it around with you forever? The answer is no. You don't, and you shouldn't. It's not healthy, and it can leave you with very little psychic energy to invest in new experiences and new people. There are many ways to unburden yourself, some of which can involve years of therapy and self-examination. What I'm going to suggest is not a substitute for this kind of work, but a simple exercise that many people find helps them feel less burdened by past experiences and the feelings and thoughts that cling to them.

This exercise is called The Container, and I use it to give people a chance to put away, at least for a time, some of the baggage of their past. It's like a storage unit for things you don't need right now, but are not yet prepared to throw out. Here's how it goes:[5]

Make yourself comfortable, close your eyes, and visualize a container of any size or material. You're going to be putting thoughts, feelings, and worries into this container, so you want it to be big enough to hold them. Make the container solid enough to hold what you put into it, and give it some kind of lock to which you alone have the key. Finally, imagine that the container has a special valve that allows you to let out some of the contents, but not all. That way, whatever you put into the container, you'll be able to retrieve whenever you want to, but everything else will stay put until you want to take it out. Once your container meets your specifications, imagine yourself loading whatever you want into it: whatever feelings, thoughts, or memories you'd like to set aside, just for a while. Now, notice what it feels like to leave behind for the time being some of what you've been carrying around.

People who like this exercise say that it helps them feel more in control and less overwhelmed. Instead of feeling like they have to deal with everything at once, they can keep some things in the container to be taken out and dealt with later.

These are just a few ways to manage uncomfortable feelings in creative ways. The next one requires a bit more time and thought, but for some people who practice it, it's a powerful source of clarity and renewal.

Creative Outlets: Transforming What Hurts

WE ALL HAVE a story to tell. If you're stuck in mourning, chances are there are holes in the story you're telling yourself, the well-worn tale that you repeat to yourself and others because that's the way the story has always been told. I did this for years with the story of my mother's death, which included details that could only have been imagined and recorded in the mind of a nine-year-old child. Embedded in my story were also a blizzard of feelings, especially feelings about being invisible and alone, surrounded by adults who were fighting off their own panic.

People have all kinds of stories and all kinds of feelings about them. The story people come to me with initially is rarely the story they leave with. Sometimes it's a matter of filling in subtle emotional shading, and sometimes it's about revising some of the core elements, reassigning responsibility, acknowledging disappointments and betrayals. It may be that what people thought was their fault was not their fault at all, or that whatever they did, they did because they had no other viable options. Often, they are left with the frustration of knowing things they could not have known at the time—risks and options of which they had been unaware. Sometimes they simply have things they wanted to say to those who are gone, and they wish more than anything that they could have just one more conversation, to say good-bye, or I'm angry, or I'm sorry, or just, I love you.

In an often-quoted study of the value of writing about painful experiences, college students were assigned to four groups: one group wrote about neutral topics; another group wrote about upsetting events but omitted mention of how they felt about the events; a third group wrote about their feelings related to an event, but not the facts of what happened; and a fourth group was told to write about both feelings and facts related to painful events in their lives.[6] Subsequently it was found that members of the fourth group consulted the College Health Center less frequently than members of the other three groups. A second study confirmed these findings and showed that the "disclosers" had less evidence of psychological and physical problems and improved T cell immune response. These results were most pronounced in students who had disclosed information about these painful events in their lives for the first time.

The authors concluded that "active inhibition of thoughts and feelings [about an experience] requires physical work and, over time, acts as an accumulative stress increasing the risk of illness and stress related problems. On the other hand, the expression of thoughts and feelings can interrupt this sequence and have a therapeutic effect." Getting something off your chest, in other words, really can make you feel better. What's more, putting it in writing has the added benefit of creating a place other than your body for these memories to reside.

Have you ever woken in the middle of the night and thought of something you had to do the next day, then lain awake, going over and over it, afraid you'd forget by morning, but too tired to get up and write it down? Only when you finally get up and put it down on paper can you relax and go back to sleep. Writing during the day can have a similar benefit, especially if there are details of a person's life or death that you are thinking about over and over again, either because you don't want to forget them or because you *can't* forget them. Some people get a journal and write out all their thoughts and feelings on a daily basis. Others find it helpful to write directly to the person who has died, sharing thoughts, feelings, and regrets that went unexpressed during the person's lifetime. Some people write a lot, and others write a page or two and find that doing so is enough to lessen the intensity of recurring worries and painful memories.

Jeane, whose sister Kathryn died suddenly and tragically, used writing in several ways. She wrote an account of the day her sister died, including all the details she had been reviewing over and over since that day. She believed she owed it to her sister to remember everything about that day, and she found relief in knowing that once she'd written the story, there was no danger she would forget any of it. That helped her think about it less. It also got her thinking more about other parts of her sister's life, and she began to write about those as well. Writing helped Jeane remember her sister as she was when she was healthy, and it helped her connect with the many happy memories that had been pushed aside by the horrible details of her sister's death.

You can give your writing a jump start by making a list: what you did together, what you miss, what you *don't* miss. Or if you're writing a letter to the person who has died, you can make a list of things you'll always love about him or her, or that you're angry about, or things you regret. You can share any of these writings with someone you trust, or you can keep them to yourself. Either way, writing is a way to get what's on the inside out into the open where it can have the benefit of light and reflection. You may find that putting your thoughts on paper makes it easier to put them aside and quiet your mind—to say, in effect, "Yes, I know this. I don't have to think about it right now."

Sharing What You've Learned: Community Involvement

ONE OF MY favorite poems begins, "Before you know what kindness really is, you must lose things" and ends, "Then it is only kindness that matters. Only kindness . . . that follows you everywhere, like a shadow, or a friend."[7] Many people who hear this poem after they have lost someone are deeply touched by it, perhaps because it alludes to one of the "gifts" of grief—the shift that occurs in people's sense of what matters most in life: to be a good person, to cherish family and friends, to value human connection. For "kindness" you could substitute compassion, or generosity, both of which Belleruth Naparsteck speaks of in describing the desires of many trauma survivors to share what they have learned with others:

> Those who recover want to serve. The man who volunteers at the Hunger Center remembers when he was in the food line, and it feels right and good to be feeding others. There is a natural, unself-conscious charity that comes right from the heart.[8]

Some people sign up for a walk to raise money for cancer, or like Jeane, to support the rights of people with mental illness. Others, like Theresa and Suzanne, volunteer to visit homebound elderly people or answer phones at a women's shelter. Someone else spends a week as a counselor at a special camp for children who've lost a parent.

What we're talking about here is not something that happens immediately after a loss; it may be a year, two, or more. Even so, the prospect of engaging in any kind of service may feel like altogether too much, particularly if you already feel overwhelmed by other people's needs. As always when you are mourning, listen to yourself, to what you're feeling. If you feel like you're giving too much as it is, maybe you need to pull back and give to yourself for a while. You may then feel that you have the energy and the desire to give to others.

But you do not have to wait until you feel energized and hopeful to take action. It's always better to do something, *anything*, than to do nothing. Finding opportunities to serve others—volunteering, raising money, speaking to groups—is often the best thing you can do to change the way you feel. It works in a number of ways. One, any kind of activity is likely to help divert you from your own sadness. Two, doing something for others tends to make people feel better about themselves. Three, helping to ease the pain of others may give meaning to your own suffering. In general, people who find ways to help others feel less despairing and isolated, more connected and useful, more a part of the world. This, too, is a form of emotional alchemy.

Joining Together: Bereavement Support Groups

I ADMIT TO having a prejudice toward reaching out to other people when you are in pain. I just don't believe that people are meant to suffer alone, or that we're built to survive without the presence, the touch, the involvement of other people. At the same time, I often hesitate to follow my own advice because I don't want to impose on other people, or because I don't want them to think that I'm needy or weak. After my mother died, a lot of people wanted to take care of me. Maybe that's why I'm always a bit wary of people's concern; it can feel too much like pity, and that only makes me feel weaker when what I need is to feel stronger.

It took me many years to overcome my natural suspicion about getting support and comfort from other people. Maybe you are a bit the same way. What I want you to know is that there are times to do it on your own, and times to ask for help. Refusing to ask for help is not a sign of strength, but another expression of the same fears that might be preventing you from addressing other aspects of your mourning. We all need other people, whether as a source of comfort, as a sounding board, or as a catalyst to help get us moving forward. Depriving yourself of that support is yet another way of denying the reality of death and its consequences.

The support of other people is important when you're mourning, for many reasons, not the least being that it's hard to open yourself up to painful emotion if there is no one there to help you handle what surfaces. It's one thing for me to tell you that you are strong enough to bear the pain of loss, and quite another to be fully present with you so that you can feel my willingness to help you bear it. It can be a loving friend or relative, a trusted religious counselor or therapist. No matter who it is, you need someone to receive your feelings, someone who can hear your words, share your pain, and help carry some of that load for you.

"Okay," you may be saying, "I've tried talking to my friends, and it hasn't helped. They keep telling me I should be over it by now. They tell me I should be getting on with my life, that that's what my husband would want (or my wife, or mother or father). Even if they don't say that, I can see just by looking at them that they're tired of hearing about my grief. I'm afraid that if I bring it up with them anymore, they're going to start running in the other direction when they see me."

There are some people who discover after they suffer a loss just how devoted to them their close friends really are. Many others are disappointed to realize that the people they thought they could depend on are not up to the task of supporting them in their grief. It's hard to accept, and yet, especially among those who have not experienced a loss themselves, death is a subject that makes people uncomfortable. They don't know what to say, they don't know how to comfort you, and most of all, they don't want to think about how they would be feeling if it happened to them (which, of course, they know it one day will). It is for this reason—the fact that people who are mourning often have a need to talk about their loss that exceeds other people's capacity to listen—that there are grief support groups.

I have led such groups for the past ten years, and I never cease to be surprised by how people who start out as total strangers can help each other through one of the most difficult times of their lives. A woman who feels devastated by the loss of her mother, a man whose sister died of cancer, a young woman whose brother died in a car accident—all different, but with a connection to each other that, at least for now, surpasses in importance any connection they have to anyone else. Their loss is what defines them, and because of that, what they need is to be with other people who understand how completely their identity, their way of life, their relationships with other people, have been altered by this one event. Groups make people feel less alone. Groups provide an opportunity for people to cry without worrying about hurting someone else, because everyone cries, at least for a while. As time goes by, they laugh, too. Most of all, they're able to be themselves, to say whatever they want to say, to express their sadness, their anger, their relief, without having it judged and without having anyone try to talk them out of it. One of the greatest rewards of the work I do is seeing people who may never have found comfort in the gentle words and presence of other people finally discover that they do not have to soldier through life alone.

So support is available, and you may find that in reaching out for it, you discover things about yourself that you may not have known. You may be surprised by how good it can feel to sit in a room with others who are not afraid to talk about their loss. You may be surprised at the strength of your connection to people you've only known for a few weeks. I often think that the bonds people form in support groups are a beautiful expression of how death, the most painful but also the most universal human experience, can bring us into closer connection with others. Seeing this happen again and again, I have come to believe that while loss can break our hearts, it can also open us to feeling more connected to others and to receiving the reassurance and comfort of their companionship.

A final word about support groups. Some are run by professionals, some are run by people with special training, and some are run by members, with no designated group leader. As with any other kind of help, you have to find a group that's right for you. The more complicated your loss, the more difficulty you are having talking about it, the more important it may be for you to find a group that is professionally run. Many groups combine people with different kinds of losses—older people who've lost spouses, young parents who've lost children, and so on. Sometimes this works, and sometimes it can be a problem, especially if some members feel that others in very different circumstances may not understand what they are going through. Ideally, you will be able to find a group that is competently run, and in which you feel comfortable talking about your loved one and your loss.

As helpful as they can be, groups also have their limitations. Many of the people you've met in this book participated in a group at some point, but they also came in for individual counseling at one point or another. There are many advantages to working with an individual therapist, and it may be the only way for you to really get to the bottom of what is interfering with your mourning.

When to Consider Professional Help

MANY PEOPLE HAVE looked at the question of whether bereavement counseling (and bereavement support groups) are necessary or helpful for people dealing with loss. The one clear finding from this research is that the people most likely to benefit from grief support are those whose mourning is the kind we've been talking about, namely people whose grief is complicated by relationship factors or by the circumstances of the death. But you don't have to try to diagnose your grief to know whether or not you might benefit from professional help. Here are some circumstances that may indicate you need extra help:[9]

- You've experienced the traumatic death of a loved one.
- You've experienced trauma in your life that the death is bringing back.
- You're showing severe signs of depression. Along with depressed mood, these include (but are not limited to) a significant decrease in interest or pleasure in almost all of your activities during most of the day, nearly every day; significant weight loss or weight gain; difficulty falling asleep or sleeping too much; fatigue or low energy nearly every day; recurrent thoughts of death or suicide. Again, it isn't necessary for you to have an in-depth understanding of depression or to try to diagnose yourself. If you think you might be suffering from depression, see someone who is trained to make a diagnosis.
- You believe over time that your grief is entrenched, is simply not letting go, not lessening, and maybe never will. If you feel stuck in your grief, you may very well be.
- You feel helpless, hopeless, or scared and those feelings aren't going away.
- You think you might need help. It never hurts to talk to someone. If you don't really need the help, a good professional will be able to reassure you of that, too.

Many people provide some kind of grief therapy or grief counseling. Like every other field, this one includes people with varying degrees of knowledge, skill, and compassion. Some therapists or counselors have degrees in social work or nursing. Some are psychologists. Some religious ministers also may be trained in counseling, and in addition religious leaders are often good resources for finding therapists and support groups in your area. Some therapists specialize in grief, but it is not essential that you find one who does. What you're looking for is someone who is comfortable talking about loss and grief, who understands the different ways that grief can become complicated, and who knows what the consequences of those complications may be. You're not looking for someone to simply hold your hand (literally or figuratively), but someone who can offer whatever kind of help you need to get you moving along the path to healing. The important thing is to reach out, to find someone who has the right qualifications and with whom you feel comfortable.

Studies of what makes for good therapy repeatedly show that the most important factor in explaining therapeutic effectiveness—more important than the type of therapy or the skill level of the therapist—is the quality of the relationship between the therapist and the person seeking help. That's a pretty powerful finding, if you think about it. People do better in therapy when they feel comfortable and safe, when they've been able to establish a solid, trusting relationship with their therapist.

I want to emphasize, again, that there's no single way to help someone who is stuck in grief. What might be helpful for one person—for example, simply encouraging a mourner to express his or her feelings about the loss—may be counterproductive for someone else who needs help managing these feelings. People who were in ambivalent or conflicted relationships may need help confronting difficult feelings, while those who were in highly dependent relationships may be better served by support in coping with the practical and emotional challenges of life on their own. People who have experienced unexpected, sudden loss need time to be able to react emotionally as well as time to think through all the implications of their loss. People whose mourning is complicated by traumatic memories may need help in extricating themselves from the hold of past events and the feelings they provoke if, as is so often the case, these feelings are getting in the way of health and healing in the present. What all this points to is that you have to find someone who is qualified and right for *you*.

Does Everyone Really Need to Talk About Their Loss?

WHATEVER WAY A person tends to operate under stress—whether to deny emotions or to dwell on them—is likely to be the way that person grieves. If people are used to shaking themselves to attention when they're sad, that's going to be their first response to loss. While it's certainly possible that they will be successful with this strategy, they may eventually want to revisit the relationship and talk about how the loss is affecting them. Or someone else may see that the person is "not herself" and suggest that she consult a grief counselor. Even a year or two after a loss, it can be helpful for someone in this situation to talk to a professional who understands the different ways that people mourn. This can be especially useful for someone who thought she was "over it" and can't understand why she is not.

But as we've seen, not everyone needs help getting their feelings out. On the contrary, someone who has a tendency to drop into her feelings and stay there is likely to have trouble finding a way back from the depths of grief. Here, too, it's advisable to see a professional who understands mourning and who can also recognize symptoms of depression and the possible need for a medical referral.

When to Consider Medication

CLEARLY, DECISIONS ABOUT medication can only be made by a competent medical professional who understands what problems you are experiencing, which of them may be related to your grief, what other complicating factors may be present, and what type of medication, if any, may be indicated. Ideally, such a person will also be familiar with your medical history and will know, for example, whether you or members of your immediate family have suffered from anxiety or depression, either of which can compound, or be confused with, grief.

The question of medication is one that frequently comes up for people who are suffering acutely after a loss, as well as for people who are not feeling any different with the passage of time than they did immediately after the loss occurred. Some people are quick to ask whether medication might help them; others are reluctant to take anything that might dull their feelings, fearing that this will interfere with their mourning. There is no doubt room for error in either direction. Most people writing about the use of medication in bereavement take the position that it probably should be considered in cases where people's coping capacities are so overwhelmed that they are having difficulty functioning: they can't eat or sleep, can't do their job or care for their families, and so on. Under these circumstances, a person may become more and more discouraged, may feel increasingly hopeless, and this in itself can make it hard for him or her to heal from the loss.

Again, while grief is not something that can or should be medicated away, there are times when the use of medication should be considered. If you are advised by your therapist to have a medication consultation, or feel you need one, I cannot overemphasize the importance of finding a psychiatrist or other medical professional who is knowledgeable about the use of psychotropic medications in connection with bereavement. If you're uncomfortable with someone, or feel that he or she doesn't want to be bothered listening to a patient whose "only problem" is that you are grieving, find someone else.

Finding Your Way

IN THIS BOOK, we've met people who were stuck in their mourning and managed to get unstuck, to begin moving again along the path of healing. We've also looked at some of the things that you or someone else might do, in general terms, to get yourself moving along this path if you think you're stuck. Now let's talk a bit about where that path leads.

As you might expect by now, this is another question for which there is no one answer. There are as many destinations as there are paths, as many paths as there are people who mourn. Still, all these paths are in one way or another part of our search for the truth of who someone was and who we were in relation to him or her. It could be said the destination is always a place where we have come to understand and accept who and what we are now that the person is no longer in our lives. With this understanding, we move off that particular life path that we call mourning and merge back onto the much broader path of growth and self-discovery that defines our life as a whole.

WHO AM I NOW? REGAINING A SENSE OF YOUR PLACE IN THE WORLD

Where does it lead, this path we all must travel? Can we ever be the same after we lose someone we love?

Of all the questions that occupy the minds of people who are grieving, to me the most poignant and universal is the question of whether they will ever be the same, whether they will ever be their old selves again. However much people may be trying to hold on to hope, when they ask this question their voice takes on a tone of sad resignation, as if to let me know that they believe they already know the answer. And in one way they are right; the only honest answer to this question is, "No, you will not be the same."

This is bound to be a sad realization, one of the many that comes with the loss of someone we love. It is particularly sad, even frightening, for many people shortly after a loss—or for those who are stuck in their grief—because the only alternative they may see to being who they were is who they are at that very moment: someone shattered by grief, a person in pieces. But in fact, as most people come to realize, there are other alternatives. No, they will not be the same as they were when their loved one was in their life. They will be different, both from the way they were before the death *and* from the way they are now. People do not go back to being exactly who they were before, but often the changes are not what they expect: some of what breaks away is old, restrictive definitions of themselves, old fears of being on their own. As they begin to reenter the outside world, they find they are opening inside as well, that they have space inside for new interests, new relationships, new experiences. So no, they will not be the same. But neither will they stay where they are. Both of these things are true.

As long as we're alive, we continue to be changed by life. So much in life cannot be anticipated, so much of what we start out believing collapses under the weight of experience. The more life challenges us to reconsider what we thought was true, the more we are changed.

When he was about four years old, my son asked me if I would be alive for all his birthdays. I said simply, "I will be alive for many, many of your birthdays, until you are older than I am now, until you have children, and then I will be alive for many of your children's birthdays. I will be alive for a very, very long time." I knew as I said it that this was more a wish than a promise. But in that moment there was no reason to burden him with concepts he could not yet absorb or to deprive him of the comforting illusion that he could be assured of my continued presence in his life. He's quite a bit older now and, like his sister, understands all too well that people die, that life offers no guarantees. He is not the same as he was. He cannot be the same, because what he knows now is more than what he knew then. His reality has changed: it is sadder, but truer. When someone we love dies, it changes us in just this way.

People ask me why their loved ones have to die, why people get terrible illnesses or die in terrible ways. I know they don't really expect me to have an answer. But still, they feel the need to ask the question, if only by way of protest, if only to let me know how wrong they think it is and to have me agree that yes, it is *wrong*. And so it is. Yet still, the fact remains. I can't take it away. No one can. So what do we do with it? How can we think of death with anything but fear and trembling, the darkness that hovers always, threatening to deprive us of what we most cherish?

> The gift that grief offers us is the capacity to see deeply the way things are. Life is limited. We are here for a short time. Grief asks us to know this, not only in a disembodied, cerebral way, but in the marrow of our bones.
> —Miriam Greenspan, *Healing Through the Dark Emotions*[10]

Can we really understand grief as a gift? It depends on our perspective. The truth is, love and grief are unavoidably interconnected. If we love, we will grieve, or die and leave someone else to grieve. If love is a gift, grief is part of that same gift. They are inseparable.

There is a book about the practice of therapy by psychologist Steve Gilligan called *The Courage to Love*. When I first picked it up years ago, I didn't understand the title. I wondered, What does courage have to do with love? What does either one have to do with therapy? Having worked for years now with people in mourning, I understand it much better. We cannot open ourselves up to another person without risk. All those whose stories we've heard in this book opened themselves to love and left themselves vulnerable to the pain of loss. This is one way in which love requires courage. Another kind of courage is involved in being willing to offer support and help to someone who is grieving: to go beyond a passive observer's stance to being a partner who steps in to help carry the burden of a person's painful feelings. There is a reason people avoid talking to people who are recently bereaved: it's unsettling on many levels, and it can leave the listener feeling helpless. If you are able to really be with someone who is grieving, to offer your human presence, don't worry about what you have to say or what you can do to make things better. What you are doing, just by being with someone who mourns, is an enormous act of generosity and love.

To remain fully present with someone who is in pain is not without risk. Listening to what another person is feeling—allowing your whole heart to open so that you can take it in, at a level beyond words—is not without risk. Most of us do this at some time or another, without thinking about it. We do it when we fall in love. We do it when we hold a child who is crying. Whenever the line between our own consciousness and that of another person blurs and we are aware that part of what we are feeling is being directly channeled from someone else, we are opening ourselves to the risk, and the wonder, of loving.

When people are circling around the same emotional territory again and again, dwelling on the same memory or feeling about themselves, it's natural to think that the way to help them is to get them to snap out of it, to try to convince them that they shouldn't feel angry or guilty, shouldn't blame themselves, and so on. But not all guilt or anger is irrational. People do hurt one another. They do make mistakes, think unkind thoughts, say unkind things, and even make bad decisions that can cause suffering and death. If you tell someone who has a rational basis for guilt not to feel guilty, the person may nod and look like he or she understands, but inside knows the truth. I think it's important to acknowledge that sometimes life lands us in situations that are beyond anything we've coped with, maybe beyond anything we *can* cope with on our own. We fail to meet our own expectations for goodness, for patience, for strength. When this happens, we have a choice. We can spend our lives beating ourselves up, or we can accept the fact that we make mistakes. Rather than thinking of ourselves as bad, we can recognize ourselves as human.

Harold Kushner makes the point that it's almost impossible to convince another person not to feel guilty: "I know; I've tried hundreds of times."

> Rather than scold the person for having inappropriate emotions, you should say to them, "I know you feel terrible about what happened, and I hurt for you. But you're a good person and I love you."[11]

What if we could say this to ourselves? What if we were able to face our fears, understand our weaknesses, admit our failures, while at the same time seeing ourselves as basically good and deserving of love?

None of the people whose stories you've read in this book had simple relationships with their loved ones. As much as they may have recognized this while the person was alive, it really was only after the person died that the relationship came into focus, like the image you see through a kaleidoscope when you stop turning it. The fragments, some light and some dark, assemble into a precise form, at least for a moment; turn it again and a different picture appears—the same pieces each time, but fractured and refracted. In the same way, memories are seen each time with slight variations, so that there is always the possibility of seeing something we haven't seen before, of seeing something in a different light. This too is the gift of grief. It is the gift of better understanding others and ourselves.

Jeane took another look at herself, and what she saw was an intelligent, sensitive woman with a desire to work hard and to give back to others. Rachael took another look at herself and saw that she could be respectful of her parents' memory and still be a grown woman with her own life to lead. Theresa took another look and saw a woman who could have been broken early in life, but who had survived, a woman who was waking up inside and feeling clearer by the day about just what kind of life she wanted to make for herself. For each of these women, for all of the people whose stories are told here, what had been a tragedy—a terrible ending—became, in time, a beginning.

Life attaches to us as we roll through it. Choose your own metaphor. We are tumbleweeds, snowballs, the sum total of what sticks to us as we move through life becoming larger and more complex. Some of what we acquire helps us survive; some of it weighs us down. Some of what doesn't kill us makes us stronger, and some of it cripples us. Much of what happens as we tumble through life is unanticipated and beyond our control.

We think of hope as the sunshine of emotions, the light in the distance that keeps us moving through the darkness, and certainly it can be that. But misplaced hope can be a siren song, a seductive distraction from the truth.

When people can't stop grieving, can't reengage with life, part of what's happening is that they can't bring themselves to let go of demonstrably false hopes: the hope that what has happened has not really happened, the hope that their loved one will return. This may sound silly, because of course, most people know that when someone dies he or she is not coming back. But it's not that simple. When a woman cries every day because she cannot speak to her mother, she is longing for return. When a man keeps everything belonging to his wife just as she left it, he is longing for return. People who are longing for return are trapped in a psychic space that draws all of us into believing that the impossible is possible: that time will not pass, that people will not get sick or old, that we will not lose those we love. To truly live without fear, we must be willing to let go of the hope that life is different from what it is.

I once gave someone a card that read, "I was going to get you a universal remote control for your birthday, but believe me, you would only have been disappointed." So much of what happens to us in life is beyond our control: is out of our hands. What is in our hands is how we manage the uncertainty of life, how we cope with the inevitable pain and dislocation we must endure as part of being human. We may even consider that the uncertainty of life is part of what makes it precious, keeps us interested, as well as a source of motivation to remain open to experiencing every moment.

I say this knowing full well that it's one thing to understand and even embrace the uncertainty of life and another to live it. I say this knowing that just when we begin to think we have accepted our lack of control, life throws us a curve to show us that we still have a long way to go. We can learn to deal with the day-to-day uncertainties of life, but when it comes to uncertainty about the big things—uncertainty about how much time we have left with an aging parent, uncertainty about the course of a loved one's illness—most of us are going to get knocked off balance, thrown for a loop. The truth is we can never be fully prepared for life, and we most certainly can never be fully prepared for death. Maybe the most we can hope for is to be open to listening to ourselves with compassion—listening to our fear, our wish that things could be different.

Listening to yourself is one thing; being listened to by someone else is another. If you are feeling helpless, ask for help. Stay connected to other people. Stay connected to life. Be aware of what you have lost, but also of what you still have. We humans are bound together as much by grief as by love, but we seldom speak of it. We need to change that, to let others know when we're in pain so that they can do the same. If there is any meaning to be taken from the terrible losses we must face in life, it seems to me it can only be that we need each other. We have to treasure the time we have with those we love. We have to stay open to love even after we have learned the hard way how much it hurts to lose those we love. If the past is never really past, then no one we have loved is ever fully lost to us. What we hold in our hearts is there forever.

To love another person is like visiting a beautiful place, a place where we are fully present and alive, even though we know that we will have to leave it sometime. The last time I was in such a place, the kind of place I visit in dreams, I stood looking out at the water and thought, I will leave part of myself here, and I will take part of this place with me. I thought then how this is true of anything I treasure and fear to lose. When someone we love dies, a part of us dies too, but it is also true that a part of our loved one stays with us. Maybe that's what the emptiness inside us is for: to make a place where our loved ones can live inside us, be a part of us, always.

May this be true for you.

Resources

There are a number of other books you may find helpful; these are a few of my favorites. For general information about death and dying as well as links to other sites, a good place to start is the Griefnet.org website or the website of the Association for Death Education and Counseling (ADEC), both included below.

Books

GRIEF IN GENERAL

Fitzgerald, Helen. *The Mourning Handbook.* New York: Simon and Schuster, 1994.

Rando, Therese. *How to Go On Living When Someone You Love Dies.* New York: Bantam Books, 1991.

CHILDHOOD ABUSE AND NEGLECT

Gil, Eliana. *Outgrowing the Pain: A Book for and About Adults Abused as Children.* New York: Dell Publishing Company, 1998.

Napier, Nancy. *Getting Through the Day: Strategies for Adults Hurt as Children.* New York: W. W. Norton, 1993.

COPING WITH TRAUMA

Lewis, Lisa, Kay Kelly, and Jon Allen. *Restoring Hope and Trust.* Baltimore, MD: Sidran Institute Press, 2004.

Naparstek, Belleruth. *Invisible Heroes: Survivors of Trauma and How They Heal.* New York: Bantam Books, 2004.

Rosenbloom, Dena, and Mary Beth Williams. *Life After Trauma: A Workbook for Healing.* New York: The Guilford Press, 1999.

LIFE-THREATENING ILLNESS

Berman, Claire. *Caring for Yourself While Caring for Your Aging Parents.* 2nd ed. New York: Henry Holt and Company, 2001.

Bolen, Jean Shinoda. *Close to the Bone: Life-Threatening Illness and the Search for Meaning.* New York: Simon and Schuster, 1996.

Dunn, Hank. *Hard Choices for Loving People.* Herndon, VA: A&A Publishers, Inc., 2001. Available from www.hardchoices.com.

SUICIDE, HOMICIDE, AND OTHER SUDDEN VIOLENT DEATH

Bucholz, Jude. *Homicide Survivors: Misunderstood Grievers.* Amityville, NY: Baywood Publishers, 2002.

Fine, Carla. *No Time to Say Goodbye: Surviving the Suicide of a Loved One.* New York: Broadway Books, 1999.

Henry-Jenkins, Wanda. *Just Us: Overcoming and Understanding Homicidal Loss and Grief.* Omaha, NE: Centering Corporation, 1996.

Jamison, Kay Redfield. *Night Falls Fast: Understanding Suicide.* New York: Knopf, 1999.

MEDITATION AND OTHER MINDFULNESS PRACTICES

Chodron, Pema. *When Things Fall Apart.* Boston: Shambhala Press, 2000.

Greenspan, Miriam. *Healing Through the Dark Emotions.* Boston: Shambhala Press, 2003.

Kabat-Zinn, Jon. *Wherever You Go, There You Are.* New York: Hyperion Books, 1994.

Kumar, Sameet. *Grieving Mindfully: A Compassionate and Spiritual Guide to Coping with Loss.* Oakland: New Harbinger, 2005.

Websites

Association for Death Education and Counseling (Adec.org)

The website for ADEC, an organization for bereavement counselors and educators, offers information about death and dying and publications on many aspects of loss, as well as a comprehensive list of Web-based resources on death, dying, and bereavement.

Griefnet.org

An Internet community of persons dealing with grief, death, and major loss. Includes fifty e-mail support groups, an extensive annotated bibliography, and many other resources.

Referral Sources

FINDING AN INDIVIDUAL THERAPIST

If you decide to seek out a group or an individual therapist, you may want to begin by talking to your physician, your friends, and others who can make a recommendation to someone they know personally. Alternately, you could begin by getting a list of providers from your insurance company and calling these providers to ask about their experience in working with grief and loss. Either way, it is a good idea to meet with a therapist to see if he or she is someone you feel you would be able to work with.

FINDING A SUPPORT GROUP

Grief support groups are often offered at hospitals and by mental health agencies. Your church or synagogue may offer a group or may be able to refer you to one. There are also specialized agencies that offer a range of groups for adults and children coping with life-threatening illness and loss. Local newspapers often run announcements for these groups. The websites mentioned provide links to national organizations that offer support groups. Some of these groups will be professionally run, and others will be peer support groups. You may want to attend more than one before you decide which is best for you.

Notes

Chapter 1

1. Based on an analysis of research on how people cope with grief, Raphael estimated that as many as one in three bereavements result in "morbid or pathological patterns of grief." If this statistic is applied to the number of deaths per year in the United States (two million) and the number of mourners affected by these deaths (fifteen to twenty million, depending on family size) this would produce a projection of five to six million new cases of complicated mourning each year. Raphael, B., *The Anatomy of Bereavement* (New York: Basic Books, 1983); cited in Therese Rando, *Treatment of Complicated Mourning* (Champaign, IL: Research Press, 1993).

2. Parkes, C. M., and R. S. Weiss, *Recovery from Bereavement* (New York: Basic Books, 1983). Follow-up to the original study and further research are reported in Colin Murray Parkes, *Bereavement: Studies of Grief in Adult Life* (Philadelphia, PA: Routledge, 2001).

3. From the play "I Never Sang for My Father" by R. Anderson, first produced on Broadway in 1971.

4. Shapiro, F. *EMDR: Eye Movement Desensitization and Reprocessing* (New York: Guilford Press, 2001).

Chapter 2

1. Rando, T. A. *Treatment of Complicated Mourning* (Champaign, IL: Research Press, 1993) 489.

2. As many models of bereavement illustrate (see Chapter 1), some degree of denial immediately following the loss of someone we love is more the rule than the exception. To accept that the death has occurred is painful. We want to avoid confronting that pain, so we put off facing reality. The more we fear the pain, the more likely we are to try to avoid facing reality. The protection we mount in our minds against confronting painful realities was labeled *denial* by Freud, who listed it among the *defense mechanisms,* so called because that's exactly what they're meant to do: defend us against what we don't want to know, defend the integrity of what we believe from the onslaught of unwanted information.

3. Drawing a distinction between healthy attachment and dependence that interferes with a particular situation and considering this alternative in deciding how she will act with recovery from grief, Rando makes this point:

> There is nothing wrong with a widow reflecting on what her husband would do in a particular situation and then considering this alternative in deciding how she will act. However, the situation would be different if she felt she must do things her husband's way. In the latter case she would be giving her husband ongoing control over her in death: *This same woman might fully recognize that her husband is dead and no longer attributes any power to him but fails to move forward in her life, preferring to live it precisely in the manner she did when she shared it with him, not making any required adaptations and not living life in a healthy way.* (emphasis mine) Rando, T. A. *Treatment of Complicated Mourning* (Champaign, IL: Research Press, 1993) 55.

4. Parkes, C. M., and R. Weiss. *Recovery from Bereavement* (New York: Basic Books, 1983) 154.

5. One way of describing this emotional back and forth is suggested by bereavement researchers Margaret Stroebe and Henk Schut, who write that the bereaved "oscillate between the pangs of grief (separation orientation) in which attention is focused on the lost person and the less dramatic but equally important periods in which energy is directed away from the loss and toward other life tasks (restoration orientation)." "Models of Coping with Bereavement: A Review" in *Handbook of Bereavement Research* (Washington, DC: American Psychological Association, 2001).

6. In the Jewish faith, *shiva* refers to the period of mourning following the death of a loved one.

Chapter 3

1. As Michael's story suggests, some of the inaccuracies may be the result of a parent's reluctance to show vulnerability to a child, or a desire to avoid letting the child know something about them that they fear would make the child angry or disappointed in them.

Chapter 4

1. According to trauma expert Bessel van der Kolk, "The actual cause of most posttraumatic suffering is . . . seeing people you love hurt each other in physical, horrifying ways." Quoted in Scarf, M., *Secrets, Lies, Betrayals: The Body/Mind Connection* (New York: Random House, 2004).

2. Relational trauma is discussed at length in Allen, J. *Traumatic Relationships and Serious Mental Disorders* (New York: John Wiley and Sons, 2001); and in Lewis, L., K. Kelly, and J. Allen, *Restoring Hope and Trust* (Baltimore, MD: Sidran Institute Press, 2004).

3. Belleruth Naparstek writes of her early attempts to help trauma survivors "talk through" their experiences: "Not only did the intensity of these episodes fail to dissipate with their retelling, if anything, they seemed to be getting worse. . .". Naparstek began to use alternative methods, in particular, guided imagery, which she found enabled people to access the nonverbal parts of their brain where fragments of traumatic memory are stored. In *Invisible Heroes: Survivors of Trauma and How They Heal* (New York: Random House, 2004).

4. See Chapter 4, "The Body Remembers" in *Secrets, Lies, Betrayals* (New York: Random House, 2004).

5. Prevalence of PTSD is higher for certain kinds of trauma (for example, 50 percent of women who are raped continue to experience PTSD symptoms three months afterward). These and other statistics on the prevalence of PTSD are reported in *Posttraumatic Stress Disorder: DSM-IV and Beyond*, Davidson, J. R. T., and J. A. Fairbank, eds. (Washington, DC: American Psychiatric Press, 1993). Maggie Scarf cites findings about gender differences in rates of PTSD (according to one study, women are more than twice as likely to develop post-traumatic stress disorder than are men). *Secrets, Lies, Betrayals* (New York: Random House, 2004) 90–91.

6. For a description of relational trauma and what motivates survivors to reenact abusive relationships, see Lewis, L., K. Kelly, and J. Allen, *Restoring Hope and Trust* (Baltimore, MD: Sidran Institute Press, 2004) 90–102. The use of alcohol and drugs as "stopgap coping mechanisms" for dealing with "unbearable emotional states" is discussed in pages 78–82.

7. Maggie Philips presents an excellent model for this type of integrated treatment in *Finding the Energy to Heal: How EMDR, Hypnosis, TFT, Imagery and Body Focused Therapy*

Can Help Restore Mindbody Health (New York: W.W. Norton & Company, 2000). Her model (SARI) involves four steps: 1) Establish *safety and stability*; 2) *activate* the psychological stressor; 3) *resolve* the symptoms; and 4) *integrate and internalize* the positive changes that have been achieved so that they can be maintained consistently. While less explicit, all of these stages are represented in the EMDR treatment sessions described in this chapter and the next.

8. This orientation owes everything to the work of Milton Erikson, whom many regard as the father of modern hypnosis. Erikson believed that clients had their own resources for healing and that the therapist's job was to help them uncover and utilize these resources. I am indebted to Stephen Gilligan for introducing me to Erikson's teachings and helping me integrate them into my practice. See Gilligan, *Therapeutic Trances: The Cooperation Principle in Ericksonian Hypnosis* (New York: W.W. Norton, 1987); and *The Courage to Love: Principles and Practices of Self Relations Psychotherapy* (New York: W.W. Norton, 1997).

9. Shapiro, F. *Eye Movement Desensitization and Reprocessing: Basic Principles, Protocols and Procedures* (New York: Guilford Press, 2001).

10. This research is presented by Shapiro and also in Zangwill, W., J. Pearson, and P. Kosminsky, "Eye Movement Desensitization and Reprocessing (EMDR)" in Shannon, *Handbook of Complementary and Alternative Therapies in Mental Health* (New York: Academic Press, 2001).

11. All competent trauma treatment begins with the determination of what approach is most likely to be helpful and least likely to produce further harm. Rothschild writes: "It is extremely important to remember that *not all clients benefit from*

work with specific traumatic memories, and some even become worse." (emphasis in original; *The Body Remembers,* p. 13.) Technical competence is a necessary but not sufficient basis for making treatment decisions. The other essential part of any treatment is the relationship between client and therapist (see Chapter 7).

12. Katherine Davis points out that resolution of traumatic experiences can only be achieved through treatments which involve reexperiencing the past, because what a person "learns" at the time of a traumatic event is state specific—connected to the particular thoughts, feelings, and body sensations produced at the time of the trauma. Changing the way a person feels about something that happened in the past requires that they return to that state—albeit in a way that is managed so that they don't feel overwhelmed. (Personal communication). Studies comparing the effectiveness of EMDR, Cognitive Behavioral Therapy (CBT) and other PTSD treatments are reported in Shapiro's book; and see Foa, E. B., T. M. Keane, and M. J. Friedman: *Effectiveness Treatments for PTSD: Practice Guidelines from the International Society for Traumatic Stress Studies* (New York: Guilford Press, 2000) 1–17.

13. Shapiro provides a detailed explanation of these procedures, including those circumstances under which it is not advisable to use EMDR, in *Eye Movement Desensitization and Reprocessing.* She also emphasizes the need for proper training in the technique and ongoing clinical supervision.

14. This phase of treatment may include the use of EMDR to strengthen these resources. *Resource installation* is the term used by EMDR practitioners for this step. EMDR protocols for resource installation are presented in Shapiro's book.

15. EMDR is a powerful technique. Training is essential not only as a means of learning the protocol and how to use it, but as

a preparation for the range of responses that can occur during processing. Just as important, training provides a basis for evaluating a client's readiness and suitability for EMDR.

16. Of course, medication is not the only way to help people feel comfortable between sessions. Any of the stabilization techniques described here and elsewhere (imagery, hypnosis) can also help a person cope with feelings brought up during processing, which in turn can help them to remain open to continuing treatment.

17. Many people have a lot of trouble taking in the love and affirmation offered to them by others. These same people may be all too ready to believe any negative comment made by someone else and to regard it as confirmation of their own view of themselves as defective and unworthy. The ability to take a step back and evaluate feedback from others is an important one, and one that can be learned. One place to begin is with Lewis, Kelly, and Allen's suggestions in Chapter 6 ("Identity") of *Restoring Hope and Trust*.

Chapter 5

1. Colin Murry Parkes provides an overview of how mode of death affects grief in Chapter 10 of *Bereavement: Studies in Grief in Adult Life*.

2. Rando, T. *Treatment of Complicated Mourning* (Champaign, IL: Research Press, 1993) 586.

3. Jeane's story illustrates how important it is not to regard grief as a uniform condition that can be treated according to a fixed set of guidelines. Differences in the relationship, and in the nature of the death, matter, and the more complicated the loss, the more they matter. In the largest study to date of treatments for complicated grief, Shear (2005) and her colleagues at the University of Pittsburgh tested the effectiveness of a

new treatment model (Complicated Grief Treatment, CGT) designed to target what were identified as traumalike symptoms relating to the death. In what the researchers labeled *revisiting* the trauma, participants were asked to close their eyes and tell the story of the death. The therapist tape recorded the story and the participant was asked to listen to it at home during the week. This technique was a modification of in vivo exposure used for the treatment of PTSD. In comparison to a group of participants who were treated with more traditional interpersonal psychotherapy (IPT) alone, those who received the combination treatment were found to have a better response. While the authors of the study emphasize that there is still much work to be done in understanding how to help people with complicated grief, this study suggests that using a treatment that directly targets symptoms of complicated grief can reduce these symptoms and promote healing.

4. The floatback technique, which links past experiences to what a person is thinking and feeling in the present, is described by Browning, C. "Floatback and float forward," The EMDRIA Newsletter, IV, 3, and in Shapiro, F. *Eye Movement Desensitization and Reprocessing: Basic Principles, Protocols and Procedures* (New York: The Guilford Press, 2001).

5. Didion, J. *The Year of Magical Thinking* (New York: Knopf, 2005) 37.

6. Ibid., 32.

7. Naparstek, B. *Invisible Heroes: Survivors of Trauma and How They Heal* (New York: Bantam Books, 2004) 338.

8. There are many kinds of traumatic death, such as homicide and natural disasters, that I have not dealt with at all in this chapter. In the Resources, I've included other books on the topic that someone who has experienced a traumatic death may find helpful.

Chapter 6

1. This is the basis of Therese Rando's understanding of complicated mourning, which she says always arises as a result of the mourner's attempt to do one of two things: "deny, repress, or avoid aspects of the loss . . . and hold on to and avoid relinquishing the lost loved one." (*Treatment of Complicated Mourning*, p. 149). It follows from this explanation that any treatment directed to helping a person who is stuck in grief must address these blocks.

2. Peck, M. S. *The Road Less Traveled: A New Psychology of Love, Traditional Values and Spiritual Growth* (New York: Simon and Schuster, 1978) 75.

3. Greenspan, M. *Healing Through the Dark Emotions* (Boston: Shambhala Press, 2003) 92.

4. Lewis, C. S. *A Grief Observed* (London: Faber and Faber, 1961) 1.

5. Rando writes: "Usually, the mourner wants to try to recapture the world as it once was. Over time, she learns that this cannot happen and slowly ceases in her attempts to bring the old world back, eases her resistance to the new world, then actively participates in the creation of that new world." Rando, T. *Treatment of Complicated Mourning* (Champaign, IL: Research Press, 1993) 427.

6. The issue here is what Rando discusses as the work of revising the assumptive world. Rando, T. *Treatment of Complicated Mourning* (Champaign, IL: Research Press, 1993) 430.

7. Ibid., 440.

Chapter 7

1. Steve Gilligan talks about how extraordinary experiences "stretch" us, calling upon parts of ourselves that are more than

what we use on a day-to-day basis: "While the Basic Levels are sufficient for ordinarily adaptive functions, the Generative Levels are needed to navigate and transform the extraordinary states of consciousness that occur, *intentionally or unwanted*, in each person's life." (emphasis mine). Extraordinary experiences "destabilize identity" (or as Jeane would put it, "blow us apart"). If we stay with the experience instead of shutting down, what awakens in us is an expansion of how we see ourselves, how we see the world, how we relate to other people. In other words, we generate new capacities for health, happiness, and healing: hence the term Generative Mind. "The Invisible Presence is Awakening" in Gilligan, S., and D. Simon, eds. *Walking in Two Worlds* (Phoenix, AZ: Zeig, Tucker and Theisen, 2004).

2. Kabat-Zinn, J. *Wherever You Go, There You Are* (New York: Hyperion Books, 1994) 3.

3. Adapted from Greenspan, M. *Healing Through the Dark Emotions* (Boston: Shambhala Press, 2003) 269.

4. If you are interested in learning more about mindfulness practices and how they can enhance your health and sense of well being, you could start with Kabat-Zinn, J. *Wherever You Go, There You Are* (New York: Hyperion Books, 1994); and see the list of Resources.

5. Described in Gilson, G., and S. Kaplan. The *Therapeutic Interweave in EMDR: Before, After and Beyond* (2000) 57.

6. Described in Pennebaker, Zech, and Rime, "Disclosing and Sharing Emotion: Psychological, Social and Health Consequences," in Stroebe, M., R. Hansson, W. Stroebe, and H. Schut, eds. *Handbook of Bereavement Research: Consequences, Coping and Care* (Washington, DC: American Psychological Association, 2001).

7. The poem is "Kindness" by Naomi Shihab Nye in *Words Under the Words: Selected Poems* (Portland, OR: Eighth Mountain Press, 1995).

8. Naparstek, B. *Invisible Heroes: Survivors of Trauma and How They Heal* (New York: Bantam Books, 2004) 338.

9. Symptoms of depression are listed in the *Diagnostic and Statistical Manual of Mental Disorders, Fourth Edition* (Washington, DC: American Psychological Association, 2000).

10. Greenspan, M. *Healing Through the Dark Emotions* (Boston: Shambhala Press, 2003) 90.

11. Kushner, H. *How Good Do We Have to Be: A New Understanding of Guilt and Forgiveness* (Boston: Back Bay Books, 1997) 60.

References

Allen, J. G. 1995. *Coping with Trauma: A Guide to Self-Understanding.* Washington, DC: American Psychiatric Press.

Allen, J. 2001. *Traumatic Relationships and Serious Mental Disorders.* New York: John Wiley and Sons.

Cassidy, J., and P. Shaver, eds. 1999. *Handbook of Attachment: Theory, Research and Clinical Applications.* New York: Guilford Press.

Chodron, P. 2000. *When Things Fall Apart.* Boston, MA: Shambhala Press.

Davidson, J. R. T., and J. A. Fairbank. 1993. *Post Traumatic Stress Disorder: DSM-IV and Beyond.* Washington, DC: American Psychiatric Press.

Fitzgerald, H. 1994. *The Mourning Handbook.* New York: Simon & Schuster.

Foa, E. B., T. M. Keane, and M. J. Friedman. 2000. *Effective Treatments for PTSD: Practice Guidelines from the International Society for Traumatic Stress Studies.* New York: Guilford Press.

Gilligan, S. 1997. *The Courage to Love: Principles and Practices of Self Relations Psychotherapy.* New York: W. W. Norton.

Gilligan, S. 1987. *Therapeutic Trances: The Cooperation Principle in Ericksonian Hypnosis.* New York: W. W. Norton.

Gilligan, S., and D. Simon, eds. 2004. *Walking in Two Worlds.* Phoenix, AZ: Zeig, Tucker and Theisen.

Gilson, G., and S. Kaplan. 2000. *The Therapeutic Interweave in EMDR: Before, After and Beyond.* Available from G. Gilson, P.O. Box 571298, Tarzana, CA 91357-1298.

Greenspan, M. 2003. *Healing Through the Dark Emotions.* Boston, MA: Shambhala Press.

Heller, D. P., and L. S. Heller. 2001. *Crash Course: A Self Healing Guide to Auto Accident Trauma and Recovery.* Berkeley, CA: North Atlantic Books.

Jacobs, S. 1999. *Traumatic Grief: Diagnosis, Treatment and Prevention.* Philadelphia, PA: Taylor and Francis.

Kabat-Zinn, J. 1994. *Wherever You Go, There You Are.* New York: Hyperion Books.

Klass, D., P. Silverman, and S. Nickman, eds. 1996. *Continuing Bonds: New Understandings of Grief.* Philadelphia, PA: Taylor and Francis.

Kumar, S. 2005. *Grieving Mindfully: A Compassionate and Spiritual Guide to Coping with Loss.* Oakland, CA: New Harbinger Publications.

Kushner, H. 1997. *How Good Do We Have to Be: A New Understanding of Guilt and Forgiveness.* Boston: Back Bay Books.

Levine, P. A. 1997. *Waking the Tiger: Healing Trauma.* Berkeley, CA: North Atlantic Books.

Lewis, C. S. 1961. *A Grief Observed.* London: Faber and Faber.

Lewis, L., K. Kelly, and J. Allen. 2004. *Restoring Hope and Trust.* Baltimore, MD: Sidran Institute Press.

Malkinson, R., S. Shimshon Rubin, and E. Witztum, eds. 2000. *Traumatic and Nontraumatic Loss and Bereavement.* Madison, CT: Psychosocial Press.

Matsakis, A. 1996. *I Can't Get Over It: A Handbook for Trauma Survivors.* Oakland, CA: New Harbinger Publications.

Naparstek, B. 2004. *Invisible Heroes: Survivors of Trauma and How They Heal.* New York: Bantam Books.

Nye, N. S. 1995. *Words Under the Words: Selected Poems.* Portland, OR: Eighth Mountain Press.

Parkes, C. M. 2001. *Bereavement: Studies of Grief in Adult Life.* 3rd ed. Philadelphia, PA: Taylor and Francis.

Parkes, C. M., and R. Weiss. 1983. *Recovery from Bereavement.* New York: Basic Books.

Peck, M. S. 1978. *The Road Less Traveled: A New Psychology of Love, Traditional Values and Spiritual Growth.* New York: Simon and Schuster.

Phillips, M. 2000. *Finding the Energy to Heal.* New York: Norton and Company.

Rando, T. 1991. *How to Go On Living When Someone You Love Dies.* New York: Bantam Books.

Rando, T. A. 1993. *Treatment of Complicated Mourning.* Champaign, IL: Research Press.

Rosenbloom, D., and M. B. Williams. 1999. *Life After Trauma: A Workbook for Healing.* New York: The Guilford Press.

Roth, G. 2004. *The Craggy Hole in My Heart and the Cat Who Fixed It.* New York: Harmony Books.

Rothschild, B. 2000. *The Body Remembers: The Psychophysiology of Trauma and Trauma Treatment.* New York: W. W. Norton.

Rothschild, B. 2003. *The Body Remembers Casebook.* New York: W. W. Norton.

Sarton, M. 1990. *New and Uncollected Earlier Poems.* New York: W. W. Norton.

Scarf, M. 2004. *Secrets, Lies, Betrayals: The Body/Mind Connection.* New York: Random House.

Shannon, S. 2002. *Handbook of Complementary and Alternative Therapies in Mental Health.* New York: Academic Press.

Shapiro, F. 2001. *Eye Movement Desensitization and Reprocessing.* New York: The Guilford Press.

Schlink, B. 1999. *The Reader.* New York: Vintage.

Stroebe, M., R. Hansson, W. Stroebe, and H. Schut, eds. 2001. *Handbook of Bereavement Research: Consequences, Coping and Care.* Washington, DC: American Psychological Association.

Vaillant, G. E. 1993. *The Wisdom of the Ego.* Cambridge, MA: Harvard University Press.

Worden, J. W. 2002. *Grief Counseling and Grief Therapy: A Handbook for Mental Health Practitioners.* 3rd ed. New York: Springer Publishing Company.

Index